The Weirding Storm
A Dragon Epic

The Weirding Storm
A Dragon Epic

Thomas Davis

To my granddaughters, Sophia and Phoebe, who have loved fantasy and poetry ever since I started reading Harry Potter to them when they were little girls.

To my grandsons, William and Joey, and especially to the music in William's soul.

To Ethel, to whom I am always indebted.

With thanks to Ray Moye and Deborah Bennison who helped edit the manuscript.

And especially to John Keats who inspired this tale after I read his long poem, *Lamia*.

Cover artwork by Phoebe Wood

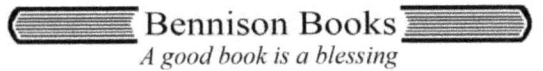

A good book is a blessing

Copyright ©2017 Bennison Books
Copyright Thomas Davis
All rights reserved
First published 2017

This book is sold subject to the condition that it shall not be reproduced in any form without the prior written permission of the author and Bennison Books. Brief quotations may be used without permission in articles or reviews.

Davis, Thomas. 2017. *The Weirding, A Dragon* Epic. UK: Bennison Books

Bennison Books Poetic Licence

978-0-9990077-0-9

bennisonbooks.com

Contents

Author's Introductory Remarks 1

Foreword 5

    Invocation to the Dragon Muse 7
    Dragonflies, Dragons, and Her Mother's Death 9
    The Old One 12
    The Coming of the Weirding Times 17
    Dreams of Fire 21
    Ruarther out of the Storm 24
    The Old One's Prophetic Dreams 29
    Inside His Room 34
    The Heat of Webbed Light 37
    Shock and the Weirding of Boundaries 40
    Ruarther's Threat 43
    Not Just a Little Girl Alone 47
    The Dragon's Conclave 50
    Weaving and Dragon Song 54
    The Substance of Light 59
    The Beginning of War 62
    Ending Dragon Community 66
    Separation in the Wilderness 70
    The Meeting of Wei and Ssruuanne 74
    Touching a Dragon's Mind 80
    Brewing Dragon War 86
    Inside a Furnace 91
    Journeying to Chaos: Search for Survival 95
    Reordering Salvation 100
    Creating a Dragon Out of Air 105
    Rising Sentience 108
    Plotting Human Extinction 112
    Escaping Possession 116
    Conversation: From Love Through Fear 121

Unexpected Warning..125
Another Dragon Scale...130
The Valley of the Scorched Black Stones 134
Doubt..137
Mmirrimann Inside the Conclave...................................141
He Called...141
Human Preparations for War 146
Vertigo and the Moment of Sudden Truth...................151
Metamorphosis..155
Determination, Doubt, and Dreams of Victory 159
Mesmerised Cave Dragons..163
The Song of Becoming a Dragon...................................168
The Mind's Black Fire..173
To War! And Raging Dragon Hearts!...........................178
The Shock of Rage..182
Fate and Sentinels 186
The Deadly Dragon Horde 190
Not the Only Enemies...195
The Dire Wolves 199
Confrontation..204
Before the End of the World..208
Retreat..211
Living Inside Chaos..215
Upon the Brink of Destruction 220
The Long Song Done..223
Being Human..227

Notes...229

Author's Introductory Remarks

The Weirding Storm, A Dragon Epic is an epic poem. Witches, dragons, malevolent spirit animals, dire wolves, hate, war, community, peace, and love spill out of the lines in a dance of words.

Written in blank verse, or iambic pentameter, it is a formal epic featuring most of the elements that are characteristic of this ancient form of storytelling which has been around since the time of *Beowulf* and *The Odyssey* by the blind Greek poet Homer. *The Weirding* includes an 'invocation' to the poetic muse, a hero's visit to the realms of death, and a story that encompasses a spirit so large it can be told only through a long poem.

Secondary epic

In his book, *A Preface to Paradise Lost*, C.S. Lewis described the type of epic presented in these pages as a secondary epic. A primary epic was oral poetry, usually performed in courts, that possessed a 'festal, aristocratic, public, ceremonial tone'.[1]

All poetry is best when performed by a skilled reader, but the primary epic brings up a vision of a great court with a large, roaring fire and a poet, or performer, sitting before an audience as he strikes his lyre and relates his epic tale.

The secondary epic is as serious as a primary epic, but neither Dante Alighieri nor John Milton wrote their great epics for performance before an audience. Milton, who became blind in 1652, had to laboriously dictate *Paradise Lost* (over 10,000 lines). Dante worked on *The Divine Comedy* from 1308 until it was completed in 1320, a year before his death.

Both poets went far beyond the unified story of a hero who embodies the spirit of a time and place, which is the substance of primary epics. Instead, they walked into the realms of God and life and death, fashioning stories that explored the fundamental questions of human existence and the central spiritual concerns of their time.

Larger than life heroes

The Weirding is a contemporary poem. It tells a wide-ranging story, mostly in traditional metre, of larger than life heroes who can be dragons as well as humans. I started writing it while reading John Keats' long poem, *Lamia*, with its strange story of a rainbow-coloured serpent that manages to persuade Hermes, the Greek god, to transform it from a serpent into a woman.

The story depicted in *The Weirding* began with an image of a young girl experiencing metamorphosis, then took on its own logic as characters and events shaped themselves into a kaleidoscope of stories that fused into an epic interrelated tale.

This work also owes a debt to Ursula LeGuin's Earthsea stories and her dragons, which have been among my favourite works of literature since I first encountered them.

This is a contemporary epic in that it does not follow a single hero from one place to another as they confront dilemmas, dangers, and barriers. Instead, it moves between the stories of Wei, a ten-year-old witch's daughter; Ssruuanne, Mmirrimann, and the rebel Shruunak, who are sentient dragons threatened with species extinction; and the villagers, Ruarther, Ruuanne, and Reestor. Nonetheless, this is a unified narrative, but one made up of many strands.

Continued relevance

In a world dominated by social media and instant communication – limited to just 140 characters in the case of Twitter – an epic poem written using traditional poetic conventions may at first seem obsolete, but the truth is that epic poetry has shaped thought and inspired men and women to feel the pulse of the universe for a long, long time. It mirrors our deepest selves.

This age, in all its confusion, is a continuation of ages past, not a separation, and the epic still has a relevant story to tell. Perhaps more so than ever.

TD, 2017

Thomas Davis had a distinguished career in American Indian higher education. He has been the president of two tribal colleges, the acting president and vice president of academic affairs of another, and the chief academic officer in two others. He recently retired as the provost of Navajo Technical University in the Navajo Nation.

He was, with Dr Verna Fowler, one of the founders of the College of the Menominee Nation and was a key player in the founding of both the World Indigenous Nations Higher Education Consortium and the Advanced Networking for Minority Serving Institutions funded by the National Science Foundation in the United States.

His book, *Sustaining the Forest, the People, and the Spirit* was published by State University of New York (SUNY) Press. He is the author of three novels and has written chapters for books published by the University of Nebraska Press and the Smithsonian. His poetry has appeared in many journals, anthologies, and magazines, including the *Wisconsin Academy Journal*, *The Lyric*, and *The Peninsula Pulse*. He also writes short stories and plays and has given poetry readings throughout the United States as well as in Canada, New Zealand, and Australia.

Foreword

Thomas Davis pays homage to the most hallowed traditions of poetry: this is storytelling, with heroes who are at once both vulnerable and courageous, with fantastical creatures and dramatic scenes, told (for the love of language) in the discipline of blank verse.

We find its essence in an early passage introducing a ten-year-old girl, whose mother has just died in their remote home, standing by a pond watching the red-eyed dragonflies and wondering how they might in turn perceive her; at the same time "*Above the house a golden dragon drove/ Great, scaly wings through heavy summer air*".

From here he unfolds a modern epic in a traditional mould. Although this has been written to be read, not heard declaimed in a great hall, we may easily imagine the poet reading it aloud to a contented gathering of the family, especially the young and the young at heart.

John Looker, 2017

John Looker's first poetry collection, The Human Hive, *takes as its theme the idea of human work in all its forms, documenting and navigating our shared history over millennia and across continents.*

Invocation to the Dragon Muse

Great dynasties exploded life in layers,
Great swarms of species split from species, swelling
Into the carnivores, plant feeders, gliders,
Free swimmers, sprinters, burrowers, a motley
Complexity of life that spread and spread
Until intelligence was brewed inside
The combinations rioting life's carpet
Across an earth of mountains, valleys, plains,
Seas, rivers, lakes, ice fields, steppes, deserts,
The cradle borning life, supporting life,
The song of meaning singing life alive.

But from this ferment of fecundity
A dark mould sends its spores into a wind.
It cleanses through a withering that wheels
Roulette-chance through the species' massive swarms.
Extinction whirls destruction's endless wheel,
And species once a glory on the earth
Depart into a nothingness where spirits
Flow through a wind that is no wind, a life
That is no life, a place that is no place.

Causation dances like a puppet jerked
By unseen strings as endings build and build.
An individual sparks against the spark
Of individuals from another species.
The wind blows withering; it blows and blows.

The question is, the question is, can mind
Unravel paths that lead toward the dance
Extinction dances as a species breathes?
Or is the dance of chaos such that darkness
Is always lurking where the mind is not?

I see a little girl and dragons as the wheel
Destruction spins whirls grim chaotic times.
I'll tell their tale if earth and wind rise up
And occupy the march of images
Spun from the words spun from the loom
That shuttles back and forth and back and forth
Into the consequence of fleeting lives.
I'll tell their tale as endings spin beginnings
And weirding slips from spectres into days
That chill the spirit with the possibility
Intelligence is not enough, is not enough . . .

Is darkness of the endless void our fate?
The warning that intelligence avoids?
Is wisdom ever in intelligence?

Come muse, come sing of darkness in the world,
The wind that is no wind, the breath no breath . . .

~ 1 ~

Dragonflies, Dragons, and Her Mother's Death

She looked at red-eyed dragonflies that hovered
Above the shining waters of the pond.
Inside the small stone house, just ten years old,
But feeling like she'd lived two lifetimes long,
She wondered how the dragonflies observed
Her hugeness when she walked out to the pond
And stared at gauze-like wings and bodies
As colourful as rainbows in a waterfall.

Above her on the mountain peaks, in caves
That joined to caves through tunnels dug by dragons,
As large compared to her as she was standing
Above the dragonflies, the noise of dragonkind
Was echoing off soaring sheer rock cliffs.
She wondered, looking at the dragonflies,
What she would feel if, suddenly, she grew
A dragon's scale-hard wings and felt the power
The dragons felt when spewing streams of fire
Out of their gut into the empty air.
She felt so small, her body thin, eyes dark
As lignite, hair as red as sunset fires.

She did not look behind her where her mother
Was stiff in death, her aging face now smoothed
Of wrinkles wrought by weeks of endless pain.

As life ebbed she had fought to stay alive
So that her daughter would not be alone
To face the coming winter's deadly storms.

At last the young girl sighed. She had her chores.
She had to dig a grave and find round stones
To place above her mother's body. She'd cried
For hours, sobs wracking through her chest, her breath
Caught up into the horror of the day,
And now, inside a weariness as heavy
As stones she'd have to find, she searched for courage.
This mountain's home, she told herself. My home.

Above the house a golden dragon drove
Great, scaly wings through heavy summer air.
A rumbling ricocheted off rocks and cliffs.
The villagers, who lived long scores of miles away
Inside their walls of stones, were terrified
Each time a dragon passed above their heads,
But she had always lived below the caves
And heard their moving, eating, talking noises.

Her mother's weight would not be much, she thought.
The stones she found would be much heavier.
She turned away from dragonflies and, careful
To keep her eyes away from where her mother
Looked up toward the dark stone ceiling's thatch,
Went through the doorway, night two hours away.

She'd manage living on the mountainside,
She told herself. She'd learned her mother's skills.
She had a woman's heart in spite of being young.
She wouldn't seek the safety of the village.
She knew how cruel they'd made her mother's life.

She went down to the shed she'd used for play
And got their spading shovel off the wall.
What should she do? She asked herself. The stones?
Or digging first? She left the shed and walked
Down to a humped-up mound above the pool.
She wasn't weak, she thought. She forced the blade
Into the mountain earth. She fought her tiredness
And lifted soil out from the hole she'd dug,
Work's rhythm balm to memory: The gasp
She'd heard her mother make as all her breath
Exhaled into a world she'd left unwillingly.

Night came too soon. Above her head a dragon
Watched silently. She laid the shovel down.
A moon as red as dragon fire rose huge
Above the jagged peaks above the cottage.
The wind was cold as evening turned to dusk.
She'd have to gather stones tomorrow morning,
She told herself and finish digging then.

She looked back at the cottage with a sinking dread.
She could not sleep outside, away from where
Her mother's eyes stared sightlessly at her.
Do what you have to do, she told herself.
You'll live through this. Do what you have to do.

~ 2 ~

The Old One

The Old One, fierce inside her double hearts,
Kept flying high above the human child
As snow whipped down from caves and
  jagged peaks
Toward the plateau where the cottage stood.

She'd sensed the mother's death and saw the girl
Construct a grave of heavy, rounded stones
And watched her as she harvested the garden,
Trapped rabbits, drying pelts outside the shed,
And fished in waters tumbling down the mountainsides.
She couldn't understand what lunacy
Infected her enough to make her notice
So small an incident as human death
And what that death meant for a human child.
A dragon tried to overlook the fact
That humans occupied the earth while dragons
Winged glory through the earth's wide sweep of skies

At night, inside her cave where hot springs bubbled
From rocky walls, the Old One's dreams were filled
With how the human girl looked facing loneliness
With dragons flying high above her cottage.
The dreams were like a fever, always there –
The human child so slight compared to dragons,
But real beyond what any child could be,
Her face emaciated, body starved,

Her eyes intense enough to be a dragon's eyes.

Each day the Old One flew above the cottage
She saw the child had made a fire and managed
To get herself through yet another night.

The humans in the valley far below
The girl stayed in their village, hunting deer
And other game, including goats the dragons
Depended on when winter howled with winds
And snow fell, burying the northern lands.
The Old One kept imagining they'd leave
Their cottages and climb the mountainside
To fetch the girl into their small stone houses . . .
But days passed, weeks passed, a month, and then
          more weeks,
The mountain peaks becoming white with snow,
And no one seemed to know about the girl.

The dire wolves started moving from the mountains
Toward the forests where the humans lived,
Starvation driving them to find new prey.
Below the dragon caves the forests waited
For storms to knife the northern winds with cold.

At last, her dreams more powerful than ever,
Her senses troubled by a hint of prophecy
That hinted at a change about to come,
The Old One swooped down on a hunter far
From where the village was, her mind on fire.
The man was bigger than most humans were.
She saw his terror as he saw her body
Above him as she rumbled through the air.
He had an arrow notched and stared at her

As wings threw shadows on the snowy ground.

"I know enough to shoot into your eyes!"
He screamed while standing tense before her scales,
Her claws extended as they touched the ground.

She snorted smoke and dug into her memory
For human words she'd learned to use against
A foolish man who'd found her lair one day.
Her honeyed words back then had brought him close
Enough to feel death fired by dragon flame.

"The plateau woman's dead," she said, her voice
As guttural as water rumbling down a cliff.
"Her child's alone and needs your human help."

The hunter's eyes glared fear and hate at her.
He looked as if he didn't know if he should flee
Or stay and fight a battle to the death.
Old, shadow memories of dragons
In skies above his head were in his eyes
From when he'd seen them as a frightened child,
The dragon-human wars a song of death.

"A child?" he asked, voice hard, fear in his breath.
He seemed to search his memory to see
If he could understand what made a dragon
Concerned about a lonely human child.

"The child above your village in the cottage,"
The Old One said. "The little, lonely girl.
She needs your help to get her through the winter."

"A little girl?" the hunter asked. His eyes grew large

As understanding dawned. "You mean the witch's child?
The one who lives below the dragon caves?"

The Old One's fires stirred deep inside her throat.
She rumbled even though she tried to still
Her double hearts to keep the hunter calm.

"What foolishness," she groused. "A witch's child?
What does that mean? A human is a human.
She is a human girl, and humans ought to care
When children face starvation's cruelty."

"Why would a dragon care about that child?"
He asked, voice straining as he fought his fear.

Ssruuanne, the Old One, eldest of the dragons,
Exasperated, snorted smoke into the air.
The hunter, frightened, drew his bowstring back
And shot an arrow at her shining eyes.
She turned her head and let the arrow bounce,
Then roared her rage and sent a spume of fire
Toward the foolish man and set his beard
To smoking as the tree behind him whooshed
Into a puff of angry, flaring flame.
The hunter turned and ran as if he'd seen
The end of time confront him in the woods.
The Old One sat and looked at emptiness.

What was a human child to her? she asked.
She'd lived through generations of the villagers.
She spread her wings and lifted into sky.
She flew above the cabin, saw the little girl,
An axe blade swinging at a chunk of wood.

You humans are a clutch of stupid fools,
The Old One thought. She flew up to her cave
And hoped she'd sleep without her troubling dreams.

~ 3 ~

The Coming of the Weirding Times

Ruarther stopped upon a ridge, the sound
Of dragon wings behind him rising, breath
So short from running that he knelt and gasped.
He'd been afraid, he thought. His mouth was dry
And stomach clenched against the memory.
He'd always told himself that if he faced
A dragon's fire he'd not give in to fear.

He could not force himself to move his legs.
Why had he turned and ran when flame had sprouted
Out of the female dragon's gut into the tree?
He'd always thought that he was strong enough
To face a dragon, look into its eyes,
And force the beast to fear his human wiles.

At last he got up off his knees and looked
At skies and snow clouds massing in the mountains.
He'd been away for weeks, the game so scarce
He hadn't even used his bow, not once.
The village needed meat. Winds gathered
And soon they'd cover forests deep in snow,
And then the herds of deer would head downhill
And hunting would become a feat of stamina.

The dire wolves, black with yellow, shining eyes
Would find the village too, their hunger bright

Inside their growls and nightly moonlit howls.
The harshness of the winter world would batter
The villagers and make them long for spring.

Ruarther stopped his musing, turned toward
The village, started running with a long, sure stride.
Ruanne, the woman that he truly loved,
But always pushed away unwillingly,
His moods perplexing, indefensible,
Would laugh to hear he'd run from dragon fire,
Confirming what she thought of him already.
He was the greatest hunter in the village.
Yet, always, gracelessness undid his efforts
To leave his bumbling tongue behind to let
Her know he loved her in his heart.
I'm coming home without a single deer,
He thought. A man without the guts to face
A dragon talking to him in the woods.

He wondered at the dragon's curious words,
The plea to save the witching girl, the meaning
Of dragons taking interest in a human life.
He thought about the witch, the cruelty
She'd faced when driven from the village years
And years ago, her husband newly dead.
She would have hated all of them, he thought.

He couldn't let Ruanne hear of his fear,
He thought. Her yellow hair and dark green eyes
Ran with him as he jogged past tree trunks massive
Inside the forest's twilit canopy.

As night grew out of shadows on the ground,
He stopped and built a fire. The winter cold

Walked like a spirit beast whose hunger burned
With restlessness, disturbing all the forest.
He took his blankets from his leather bag,
Edged close to where the flames danced merrily
And closed his eyes, sleep letting him forget
The dragon, witch's girl, his fear, his dread . . .

Before the sun had risen over mountains
He woke. He smelled a bear. He grabbed his bow.
The world was silent. No bird song, no breeze . . .
And then he saw a bear so huge it seemed
As if it were the spawn of dragons, brown
And shaggy in the darkness, dangerous,
Eyes glowing in the moon's dim silver light.
Its eyes looked straight into Ruarther's eyes.
A weirding chill iced deep inside his head.

The great bear stood on hind legs eight feet tall.
It made no sound, but stared and stared at him.

And then, inside his head, a rumbling voice
Said, "Humans should beware of dragons' minds."
Ruarther touched his ears and shook his head;
There was no way he could have heard a sound.
No natural bear had speech like dragons did.

He looked around. Light crept through trees.
He thought he heard the warning of a growl,
But when he looked back at the bear, the bear
Was gone, and birds were singing to the sun.
He sensed the snow clouds not yet in the sky.

The witch's child! He thought. The dragon, then
The bear! Strange happenings that had a pattern,

The same as if Old Broar had cast his bones
And saw the future through his cloudy eyes.
It had to be the witch's child aligning
The universe against the village peace,
Her mother's hatred blooming in the child.

A good-sized doe walked through the trunks of trees
Not fifteen yards away. Without a thought
He notched an arrow, let it fly at her.
She startled, leapt, crashed dead on ground. He'd hunted
A week, and now he'd found his prey and felled it.
Rejoicing flooded through his thought . . . but then
He smelled the bear's rank smell, the coming storm.

He'd have to warn the villagers, he thought:
Old Broar, Ruanne, the village leader Reestor . . .
He'd not been brave, but still, the portents swirled
About him through the trees, the shivering
That made him feel as if he'd drowned in floods
From rivers clogged with chunks of floating ice.
Awareness of the shivering sparked like
The fear felt looking in the dragon's eyes.
He'd have to run through several long, hard days.
Strange times were on them, weirding times.

~ 4 ~

Dreams of Fire

Wei sat inside the cottage by the fire
    And wove light strands into a radiant web
    That glinted firelight back toward the flames.
She moved her hands and thought about her mother
Beside the fireplace, weaving gentle spells,
Her daughter learning as she watched her hands.
The web threw light into the darkest corners
And made the cottage haven safe and warm.
Strong winds blew sleet against the walls and roof.

At last she let the strands of light go dark
And got up from the floor and walked to look
Outside into the storm's cold, deadly fury.
She thought about her mother's face before
Her sickness took away her strength. Her pale,
Green eyes had always danced with light, her smile
So bright it banished hurts that made Wei cry.
In storms her eyes would grow intense, alive
To clouds that sailed with lightning, dragging fire
Beneath their rumbling through a summer's skies.

Wei sighed and shivered. Frost had caked the window
And only left a small round hole to see
White wind ghosts walking over frozen ground,
Their fleeing emblematic of Wei's life.
Wei's loneliness was sharp enough to burn
Into her flesh, her sadness like a mask

That covered every inch of who she was.
She thought about the moment by the grave
When numbness made her silence all encompassing,
Her heartbeat stilled to nothingness.

She'd thought about the humans in the village.
Beside her mother's grave, her work to bury
The only person in the world she loved, she'd wept.
She thought of walking down the mountainside
And saying she was not a fearsome witch.
She'd been so tired from piling stone on stone
To make a mound above her mother's grave,
But then she'd felt the mountain stir its rock
And touch her spirit with a spirit old
As water splashing over mountain stones.
I won't need them, she'd thought. They'd chase me off.

She vaguely had a sense of angry faces
And children throwing stones that struck her mother,
A tiny girl behind her mother scared . . .

But by the window, looking out at winter,
She shook from loneliness and all the gloom
She'd felt each day she'd been without her mother.
She thought about the dragons in their caves,
The way they lived their lives together, bound
By memories and happenings that flowed
Into their flights above the cottage, sang
Into their daily voices as they linked
The way each dragon was into community.

She dreamed while standing by the windowpane
About a golden dragon looking fiercely
Into her eyes and saying, "Yes, you'll do.

The elders won't object to how you've grown."
And then she felt herself spread wings of light,
Made of the light she'd strung into a web
Beside the cottage fire, and lift into the air.
Her cottage was below her as she flew
Toward the human village in a rage of joy.

The vision dimmed. She shivered, turned away
From wind that howled at wind ghosts in the storm,
And went back by the fire that needed wood.
She felt the dullness of her hunger burn
Beneath the burning of her loneliness.

"I'll be a dragon." In her voice she sounded sure.
She looked at arms that had become too thin
As rabbits had become aware that she
Was not as skilled at calling as her mother.
She saw them scurrying about, but when
She tried to mimic how her mother sang
Them softly to the traps she'd made of willow,
They hopped away from her into the brush.
She wondered if she'd ever feel alive
With happiness the way she'd felt before.
She settled by the fire and watched the flames.

~ 5 ~

Ruarther out of the Storm

One

Ruarther stopped inside the meadow, dread
A tingling pain behind his head and neck.
The doe was heavy on his back, but pliable,
A coat whose legs stuck out with black, sharp hooves.
He turned to look behind him at the forest.
White clouds were moving fast across the fields.
A wall of mists glazed ice across the ground,
A line dividing ground and brutal cold.
Behind the line the world was icy white
And moving at the place he stood where earth
Was brown and looked as if it still was fall.
Dismay and disbelief shrilled through his arms.

The weirding! In his mind he saw the bear
Rise up inside the forest as he woke
And heard its roar imbedded in the wall
Of brutal cold and ice that slid toward
The place he stood. The witch's spawn! he thought.

The mist rolled over him. Ice covered skin.
He felt as if he'd never move his legs again!
They stung from freezing pellets in the clouds.
The dragon that had brewed his fear in vats
Prepared by witching words and weirding vials
Was in the mist, the glazing shields of ice!
The cold was brutal as it stung into his flesh.

The witch's child, he thought. The witch's child

He forced himself to turn toward the village.
The doe had frozen hard around his shoulders,
One moment pliable; then frozen stiff.
What will we do? he asked himself. A moan
Rose from the trees behind him as a fierce,
Sharp wind that stung his ice-encrusted face
Drove snow across the meadow's emptiness.
He forced himself to move. He wondered if
He had the strength to fight the wind and snow.
He'd never faced a weirding storm before.
He forced himself to run. He felt a fear
Like that he'd felt when facing dragon flame.

Two

The hunters came out of the angry storm
One at a time, beards caked with ice, hands burning
From bitter cold. Each one, dejected, sat
Inside the village hall and said they'd seen no game.
Their families needed meat, but as the storm
Had threatened, animals had disappeared.
At last the men were home, except for one:
Ruarther always brought back game no matter
What weather howled or animals retreated
To lower altitudes or hidden dens.

As Reestor donned his bear-hide cloak to walk
Toward the stone walls at the village edge,
He thought about the times starvation stalked
The mountain folk until their greatest hunter
Came bearing meat enough to keep their bellies
From shrinking during long, cold winter nights.

The hunts had not found game for much too long.
An illness seemed to stalk and blight the north,
And now the winter, when grim scarcity
Would stalk the village like a beast, had come.

Still, no one liked Ruarther – even though
His generosity was greater than
That shown by any other village man.
His pride was harsh as acid; when he spoke
He made his fellow hunters, even Reestor, flinch.

Ruanne, desirable to all the men,
Kept all of them at bay and let them know
Ruarther was the only man for her,
But even she was challenged when she tried
To soften haughtiness enough to let
Love's light shine through her eyes into his heart.

Outside the wind blew blasts of heavy snow
In Reestor's eyes. He leaned into the wind
And took forever crossing to the wall
A hundred yards from where the village hall
Stood solid in the shrieking storm. He stood
Beside the oak wood gates that barred dire wolves
From cottages and stared into the snow.
The storm was three days old and still as fierce
As dragon mothers sheltering their young.
He knew Ruarther's strength and skill, but still . . .

The big man teased the headman's blinking eyes.
The snow clouds cleared, then billowed white again,
A glimpse of brownness shouldering fresh meat:
Salvation from the promised days of hunger.
The old man felt triumphant as the wind

Shrieked like a demon from a dragon's fiery gut.
He shoved the gate while kicking at the snow,
The snow too deep to let the gate swing open.
Ruarther, face around his eyes raw, red,
Turned sideways, slipped inside the gate, and grunted.
He looked exhausted as he let the doe
Fall to the ground, its carcass frozen stiff.

As Reestor grabbed Ruarther, keeping him
Upright, the big man's eyes locked on Reestor.

"The witch is dead," Ruarther croaked. "Her child
Is stirring up the dragons, witching them.
We need to organise ourselves for war!"

The wind began to roar as if the sky
Was threatening to tear apart their lives.
Ruarther, Reestor stumbled through the wind.

The dragons? Reestor thought. They'd been at peace
With men for years. The witch had lived
Below them peacefully without a problem.
No villager need fear a dragon war.

The memory of how the witch had left
The village troubled him, but then he staggered.
He felt Ruarther's weight. The strongest man
He'd ever known was stumbling like a child.

"The bear," Ruarther mumbled incoherently.
"I heard the bear warn of the dragon child."

Relieved, the village hall now looming, Reestor
Felt, blasting through his body, cold and chills

That shrieked into his spirit, endless cold . . .
He reached the hall's stout door and pounded hard.
His strength was gone. Ruarther squared his shoulders
As light spilled from the hall into the snow.

~ 6 ~

The Old One's Prophetic Dreams

The Old One flew past layer after layer
   In dreams so vivid that they seemed to smell
   Of humans sweating in their meeting halls.
The hunter she had found out in the woods
Was pacing like a spirit bear whose rage
Had left the spirit world and slipped inside
The human by the great stone fireplace, hands
And gestures punctuating madness, fear.
He could not feel the spirit haunting him.

"The witch's child has stirred the dragons up!"
The big man roared. "The time for peace is done!"

The Old One twisted, tossed upon her bed.
The storm outside was raging, winds so strong
They moaned across the peaks and slammed down slopes
Into the valley where Wei slept in bed.

She'd riled the hunter up. Infected by the fear
She'd thrown at him with fiery breath, he'd lost
His sense of who he was and snarled in anger.

"Ssruuanne! Ssruuanne!" Her daughter's rumbling voice
Cut through the layers of her dream and forced
Her from the village back into her cave.
She opened eyes and saw her daughter's eyes.
They whirled with azure in their emerald depths,

Their spinning emblematic of her fright.
The dream still heavy in her mind, she blinked,
Then stretched her golden neck in winter air.

Mmlynn has gotten larger than I am,
She thought. Or else, she smiled inside, I've shrunk.
"What's wrong?" she asked, her voice so loud it echoed
Inside the hollow of the stone-walled cave.

Her daughter's eyes kept staring at her, making
The Old One feel unnerved by youth's strong passions.
Her daughter looked toward the tunnel dug
Between the Old One's outer lair and caves
That honey-combed into the mountainside.

"Your roaring woke the dragonlings," she said,
Then paused . . . "and others in a dozen lairs."

"I've been asleep," the Old One said. "I've roared?"

"You've dreamed?" her daughter asked, dread in her voice.
Ssruuanne looked out into the violent storm.
"I've heard you for a month," her daughter said.
"Tonight it's gotten out of claw and tooth."
She paused, her sense of dread so strong it filled
The air inside the cave. "Prophetic dreams.
You're having dreams foretelling tragedy."
She paused, then added quickly, "Everyone
Inside the mountain knows what's going on."
The Old One looked into her daughter's eyes.
Prophetic dreams could stir the dragon spirits,
Unsettle life inside the mountain, force
Change, roaring, belching fire, into the world.
She slowly got up from her bed and felt

The aches of old age deep inside her bones.
Had Mmirrimann heard of her nightly dreams?
She wondered how her ancient lover's mind
Would wrap itself around unsettling news.

"We need to bring the human girl up here,"
She said. "I'm dreaming of the human girl."

A tiny ball of flame puffed from Mmlynn.
Shock stunned into her eyes and azure face.
"She'd die up here!" she said, her voice severe.
"No dragon's ever let a human climb
Within a mile of any outer cave!
The males would murder her before she drew
A single breath inside a single lair!"

The Old One walked toward the opening
To look into the storm that moaned and raged
And danced with snow ghosts large as dragon bodies
Down cliffs and plummeting, long slopes of rock.

"I know," she said into the moaning wind.
"But change has come, and dragonkind will change,
Or else the village humans will become
Like ravers with a rage too strong to stop."
She paused, her voice so strong it magnified
The noise the wind made as it swept up snow.
She turned back to her daughter, forcing down
The roaring in her voice. "The girl is strong,
But weak," she said at last. "I've tried to stop
The dreams, but every night they're more intense."

Mmlynn kept staring at her mother. Dreams
By dragons that had lived so long, that came

From layers far below their consciousness,
Could never be ignored. Their prophecies
Came massing from the minds of all the dragons
Inside the mountain's winding tunnels, caves,
From generations who had long since died.
Somehow the old ones knew substance still
Alive from dragon generations streaming
Back through the ages of times dead and gone.

Once, long ago, each dragon had lived inside
A solitary world, its greed for gold
And other gems so great it could not dream
Of living near another dragon's lair,
But when Areetheea and Gorgon found
Each other, they had changed the universe,[2]
And in that change were dreams that dragons dared
Not disregard as imminent calamity
Hung like extended claws above their lives.
Her mother, even when she'd been too young
To be a dragon dreamer, had had dreams.

"We'll need a conclave then," she said, her voice
So small it disappeared into the air.

Ssruuanne looked at the remnants of the dreams.
"They'll want to kill the child," she said, her question
Of why she cared posed when the hunter fled
Still in her voice. "When frightened, every life
delivers death to try to stay alive."
Mmlynn turned back toward her dragonlings.
"They will," she said. "No matter what you say."

She left. Ssruuanne turned back toward the storm.
How could the child survive? she asked herself.

Alone, a winter worse than any one before,
The village humans building rage against
A human child they had not even seen —

She turned back to her bed. What could she do?
She asked. What magic did the child possess?
What madness plagued her through unwanted dreams?

The storm would end, she thought. It had to end.
And then? The question settled in the cave.

~ 7 ~

Inside His Room

The fever left Ruarther as days passed.
The fever of the dragon's flame still burned.
It blazed eternal, fire that could not end,
But flesh began to heal from illness caused
By days of walking through the weirding storm.

The storm outside was still a blaze of cold
And endless snow and wind that seemed related
To all the fevers waking him each night.
The great bear in the woods kept rising up
And speaking human words, its eyes a fire
As hot and bright as flames from dragons' mouths.
He got up from his bed and paced and paced.
Inside the hall he could not speak to those
Who greeted him. He stared at them as if
They were an emptiness he could not see.

Ruin walked the world. He felt the coming ruin.
He tried to speak the prophecy he felt,
But every time he spoke the words were wrong,
And so he went to bed at night and tossed
Upon his narrow mattress, frightened, angry,
Determined that he'd save the villagers
In spite of how they turned away from him,
Avoiding looking at his feverish eyes.

Ruanne kept trying to engage him back

Into the village's community,
But every time he looked at her he saw
How she would look when dragons spewed their flame
At her and took away her flesh from bone,
Her loveliness charred black; her heart dark smoke.
He saw her skull stare sightlessly at him.

They didn't understand, he told himself. They went
About their lives and couldn't see the nightmare
The witch's child was brewing near the caves
Where dragons plotted war against the village.
They were his people, but were blind to how
The dragon landed by him in the forest
And spewed its flame and woke a spirit bear
And let it walk about the earth unhindered,
Its haunting driven by a witch's spells.

He tried to tell Ruanne, but she had looked
As if he'd lost his mind and did not know
How badly he'd been injured by the storm.
Sometimes he walked out of the room and stood
Beside the door and listened to the wind.
Its weirding stirred him with a rage so fierce
It made him see the path toward the cliffs
He'd have to trod to keep the village safe.

I have to kill the witch's child, he thought.
The storm had made him weak and sick, he thought.
The revelation turned his stomach inside out.
I have to kill or watch the dragons stirred
Into the ancient dragon rage of war.
I've got to stop her saying spells that stir
Up spirit beasts and dragon double hearts.
She is a child, but evil has to die.

At meals he walked into the dining room
And tried to speak, but could not speak, his tongue
Encumbered by his fears and silent rage.

~ 8 ~

The Heat of Webbed Light

The snow kept falling for another day.
   Wei looked at wood piled up inside the bin
   And thought about the difficulty facing
Her if the wind kept growing drifts of snow.
At times the wind died down as giant flakes
Came drifting from the skies, and, looking out
The frost encrusted window by the door,
She saw how deep the drifts were piling up.
Each time the blizzard winds died down, they started
Again, ferocious, constant, howling rage.

As evening darkened skies, her nervousness
So great she felt half sick, she pushed the door.
It did not move, the snow too dense to move.
She strained to open up a crack. She stopped
And tried to force the panic rising up
Inside her chest to calm into her thoughts.
The snow was piled too high for her to move.

What could she do? She had potatoes still . . .
She would not starve, but wood! Beside the shed
Her daily work had built a high, square pile,
But if the drifts imprisoned her inside,
The fire would turn to ash and cold. What then?
She put her back against the door's harsh cold.
What then? The question froze her arms and legs.

She had not cried since burying her mother,
But now she felt as if she were a little girl
Who needed comfort, needed mother's love.
Her body heaved from sobs that made her shake.
The fire would die without more wood to burn.
The cold could be as deadly as the teeth
Of dire wolves ravaging their hopeless prey.
She wailed aloneness, fear into the night.

She forced the sobs to end. She could have walked
The mountainside to stone-built houses, walls,
But living in her dreams she'd thought her strength
Could let her stay beside her mother's grave.
The villagers could be as frightening
As cold, she thought, and every bit as cruel.
She got up from the floor and put a log
Into the embers red with dying flames.

And then, behind her and the fire . . . She turned.
The firelight dancing on the wooden floor,
She saw no source for noise. Her skin crawled, tingled . . .

Beside her mother's empty bed the darkness
Seemed solid, like a pool that shimmered substance.
Wei stared into the darkness, opened up
Her mouth and tried to scream, but silence swallowed sound.

Inside the pool of darkness, small, intense,
A light began to grow. Wei held her breath.
Her mother's body, lined with pulsing light
Upon the narrow bed where she had died,
Began to weave her graceful arms and hands.
Wei gasped, her sudden grief subsumed by awe.
Her mother here? The storm outside so fierce?

The light glowed like her mother's gentle smile,
And then an unreal darkness swallowed light;
Then darkness was the darkness of the night.

The sudden disappearance of the light
Hit Wei as if a fist had slammed her stomach.

The fire behind her felt as if the dark
Had fed its flames and made the cabin bright.
Wei straightened, looked into her hands, and saw
Her mother's motions as she moved as light.
Wei walked, entranced, toward the window.
She made the pattern from her mother's hands.
A web of burning light flowed from her fingers
Through window glass into the howling dark.
Her hands felt warm, as if the light she webbed
Through glass into the night was more than light.

The crusted frost upon the windowpane
Evaporated in the freezing dark.
Wei stopped the movement of her arms and hands.
Her mother, buried under snow, had given her
Survival from the storm, she thought. Her life.

The door would open as she moved her hands.
She'd melt a path to get more wood come dawn.
She'd melt the piles of snow upon the wood.
She had to think about the webs of light.
Her skill had uses she'd not understood.
She felt so tired she wondered if she'd stay
Awake enough to keep the fire alive.

~ 9 ~

Shock and the Weirding of Boundaries

Ssruuanne's long neck jerked up into the air.
Outside the storm still raged and howled with winds.
She was awake; prophetic dreams had fled.
The human girl was watching as her mother
Used hidden lines between the waking world
And universes where the shadows swarmed
In patterns sibilant with singing winds.
The daughter's hands spewed webs of light.
A dance of heat ran through the webs and burned
Through cold and snow as if they'd never been,
Exposing ground beneath the piles of snow.

The Old One's golden eyes expanded, whirled
While power flowed into the human girl.
It was a dragon's power, power drawn
From blood more ancient than the blood of dragons
That lived inside community inside
The caves dug deep into the mountain's heart.

Ssruuanne's two hearts were beating with a force
That seemed to echo through the caves and tunnels
Where dragons waited out the storm so they
Could climb on ledges, launch into the air
To hunt for mountain goats and sheep and deer
Now hunkered down, protected from the storm.

How could she see with second sight awake?

Where did the power now inside the girl
Originate? What did it mean? What force
Had mother's love sent from the realms of death?

A long, low wail lunged from the unseen peaks
Above the cave and rolled with fearsome winds
So filled with shards of ice it seemed as if
The mountain's face would sheer away, and leave
A grinning skull of gaping mountain bone,
Into the valley where the human girl
Turned back toward the fire that threw its warmth
Into the cottage's deep darkness, air
Alive with possibilities not known before.
Appalled, her pounding blood a double beat
That sang the history the dragon race
Had lived inside the shining web of time,
The Old One stared into the stormy darkness.
The human girl was linked to her, she thought.
Linked somehow deep inside her dragon blood.
She'd known the mother, but had never thought
About the woman living in the valley.
She'd been a presence banned from humankind
That lived her life below the dragon caves.

The Old One's blood was boiling contradictions,
A moving tapestry of fear, hope, rage, delight . . .

There were no walls between the universes.
They never touched except in tiny whorls
That knitted all that was together, bound
By actuality, the mind of God.
The weirding of the storm and darkness raged
Inside the webs of light the young girl wove.
Ssruuanne, the Old One, stared and stared at where

Her cave led out into the storm and dark
And felt the gusts that blew into her den,
Her long neck rigid with a dragon's fear.

~ 10 ~

Ruarther's Threat

As Reestor glared at him, Ruarther felt
As if he'd turned to stone, his spirit hard
And eyes as cold as when the wall of ice
Had overtaken him inside the field.

"We've been at peace with dragons much too long
To start a war with them," the old man said.
"You're dreaming's not enough to have them fly
Above us as their breaths char all we love."

They stood beside the fireplace in the village hall.
Ruarther had, at last, with Reestor there
And over half the village and Ruanne,
Gathered up his silence, shattered it
With words, and told his witches, dragon tale.
He felt as if he had to warn the village, speak
The dangers that he saw, or, like before
The dragon, let his cravenness rule his spirit.

"It was no dream," Ruarther growled, his temper blazing.
"The dragon singed me with her stream of fire!
I felt a dragon's fire across my head!
We have to kill the witch's girl, or else
The world will change in ways that weird us all!"

Ruanne, disoriented, looked at her only love.
He'd kill the child? She'd dreamed of having children

Since childhood, playing with her handmade dolls.
What child had powers strong enough to cause
Grown men to quail before their unlived lives?
She tried to see inside Ruarther's rage.
A hundred times she'd thought she'd earned his love,
But every time he'd danced away from her.

"Why do you meld the dragon with the child?"
A stubborn Reestor asked, eyes fixed on rage.
The man was weak yet, still affected by
The storm he'd barely made it through to home.

Around them villagers stood listening,
Their argument an awful bane when winter
Was harsh enough to threaten all of them.

"The dragon spoke about the child," Ruarther spat.
"Why wouldn't they be linked? She spoke of her.
If not from spelling by the witch's child,
Why would a dragon speak again to men?"

Old Molly grasped Ruanne's slim hand and hissed.
"You're young, young man," she said. "Your blood runs hot
Or else you would have known what good is yours.
You're foolish. In the past we fought the dragons,
And many died. Back then the dragons seldom
Attacked unless they were alone, but now
They have communities just like this place.
If stirred, they'll come together in a clan."

Ruanne felt like she ought to scream the swirl
Of roiling feelings trapped inside her chest.
She saw the anger blaze into the hunter's eyes.

"The storm is done," Ruarther said. "I'll go.
It doesn't matter what the village thinks.
I see the danger rising in a cloud,
And like I've brought back game when others failed,
I'll save the village from temerity.
The weirding's got to stop. The girl is dead."

Ruanne heard children laughing in the snow.
The storm was over. Now they'd laugh and sing.
The young could always banish clouds as soon
As sunshine sparkled on new fallen snow.
Inside her mind she felt the dragons flying
In multi-coloured clans, an endless stream
Of fire and deadly claws out of their caves.

"I'm leader still. Not you, not yet. You won't
Go up the mountain," Reestor said. "We need
More meat. The hunters have to hunt for game."

Ruarther glared at him. He glanced at Brand,
The hunter nearest him in strength and skill.
The hunter looked away as if he'd heard
His young ones as they worked to dig a path
Between the cottages through feet of snow.
At last Brand looked into Ruarther's eyes.

"No hunter has your strength or skill," he said.
"You need to throw your madness out and be
The leader that you've always been for us."

"Nobody understands," Ruarther said,
His bitterness a rancour in his voice.
He turned and looked toward the hall's great door.
He looked at Reestor. "I have always done

What's good for all of us," he said. "I'm certain
Deep down that what I'm doing's for the best."

Before the men around him moved, he strode
Toward the door, his face implacable.

Ruanne took flight outside her thoughts, her feelings
As raw as skin upon the head of children
Brought out into the light outside the womb.

"You're wrong," she heard herself say, voice as sharp
As sharpened knives. "You cannot kill the child!
To kill a child forever marks the soul
With blackness stained into an evil life."

How come he always stirred her tongue to sharpness?
Ruarther stopped and looked into her panicked eyes.

"I'll love you all my life," he said, voice loud.

He groaned inside to see the pain that shocked
Into her eyes, his words a flight of arrows
That knocked her back, away from what he felt.
He turned, picked up his bow, plowed through the snow
Toward the stone wall built around the village.

Inside the hall a hunter, Cragdon, startled,
Then left the hall to join Ruarther's rage.
His young wife grabbed at him, missed, wailed with fear.
The young man did not stop or even pause.

~ 11 ~

Not Just a Little Girl Alone

One

The morning light spilled on the floor and woke
    Wei from a dreamless sleep. She yawned and
        stretched,
Got up into the cold of early morning.
She stoked the fire to take the chill away,
Then fried potatoes on the stove before
She shrugged into her heavy coat and stood
Before the door, her heartbeat loud, hands still.
She felt her mother's hands move through the air.
She let her hands move like her mother's hands.
Light jumped into the early morning light.
Outside a hissing sound steamed through the air.
Wei stopped the motions, pushed against the door.

A wall of snow confronted her beyond
The space her light had made around the door.
She started weaving hands again, the light
Streamed from her fingers in the frigid cold.
Snow turned to steam, a whiteness hissing up
Into the morning's crystal clear blue sky.
The door swung open when she pushed on it.
She walked toward the wood pile, open ground
Materializing as she slowly walked.

She felt triumphant, filled with victory.
The storm was gone, and she could make a path

Through seven feet of hard packed, drifted snow.
She'd make it through the winter storms and cold.
She was not just a little girl alone.

Two

The Old One, tired from lack of sleep, went out
Onto the ledge outside her cave and launched,
her wings alive to updraughts in the air,
Her eyes so deep with seeing that the universe
Throbbed blazing morning light around her head.

She flew above the cabin where the girl
Was steaming snow into the morning skies.
The sight of magic shining in the sun
Unsettled her; the girl unsettled her.

A moment later, higher in the sky,
She saw two hunters, with their snowshoes sunk
Into the sweeping plains of drifted snow,
Strain up the mountainside, the snow too deep
To let them make the three-day trek to where
The human girl was gathering her wood.
She felt their violence as they made their way
Toward the girl who'd freed herself from death.
They'd be at least a week at struggling
Up slopes that steepened, rising into mountains.

She wondered how she knew the men's intent.
What should she do? She asked herself, disquiet
A power in the steady beat of wings.
What madness had the girl brought to the world?

She swooped toward the hunters, forcing them

To see her hurtling from the shining skies.
The hunters stopped and looked at her, dismay
And fright stunned through the way they stood and looked.
The one she'd singed held up his arm and fist.
She tipped her wings and soared toward the mountains.

She flew above the cottage where the girl
Was loaded down with heavy chunks of wood.
She swooped so low she had to swerve to miss
The cottage roof, her whirling, golden eyes
Locked deep into the girl's small human eyes.

Wei did not flinch or turn her head away,
But looked into the Old One's eyes, a question
Unsaid inside her look. Ssruuanne soared high
Toward the mountain peaks again, toward
The places where the wind blew unabatingly
In fierce intensity and moaning rage.

Three

Wei felt the dragon's wings before she saw
The eyes that coldly bored into her mind.
She felt intelligence inside the glare.
She stood and watched the golden dragon fly.
She fought to memorise the dragon's shape
And how it felt inside its golden eyes.

Four

Inside the moaning winds the Old One sent her thoughts
Toward the human girl. Run child, she thought.
The hunter has his cunning and his bow.
The dragons have no love for humankind.
Child, run and hide, she thought. From all of us.

~ 12 ~

The Dragon's Conclave

Sruuanne's claws touched the ledge. The summons came.
She did not hesitate, but walked toward
The tunnel that would lead into the mountain.
She felt the gathering that moved before
Her through the caverns, tunnels, endless caves.
The movement of the mountain dragons seemed
More powerful than any storm the world
Had borne throughout its endless history.

She blanked her mind from thought and dream.
She hardly saw the other dragons as she joined
Into a stream of colours walking through
The ghostly lights the young ones mined from veins
Of crystal near the mountain's granite cliffs.
The thunderous noise of dragons walking hummed.
The young girl's eyes kept flickering and shining
Inside her consciousness. It made no sense,
But in her blood she felt the young girl's heart.

The dragons parted as she walked into the cavern,
The sea of necks and spines, the glittering of eyes
Electric as a thousand lightning bolts.
Mmlynn's bright eyes watched as her mother walked
And flinched to see her mother's absent eyes.
Her mother looked as if her nightly dreams
Had entered day and burned with unwilled fire.

Ssruuanne walked up toward the round, black dais
Where eight huge elders sat, their whirling eyes
Upon her as she did not hesitate,
But climbed the nine huge steps to tower over
The conclave's rumbling, restless energy,
The eldest of the eldest of their race.

Upon the dais she turned to dragons she
Had known since they had quaked inside their eggs.
She was the oldest. Still, the eight had lived
Through years of war with humans, then the moment
When dragon isolation ended deep
Inside this cavern in the mountain's heart.

Old Mmirrimann looked deep into her eyes,
The dragon that had changed the fate of dragons,
His dark green eyes a swirl of radiance.
He turned his head toward the dragon sea.
Ssruuanne's eyes swept toward the ceiling where
The spoils of other ages were embedded
In melted stone, old gold and jewels long
Ago discarded, then looked down at silence
As dragon eyes stared at the place she stood.
She felt the bristling of thought and fear inside
The minds behind the eyes, the wondering . . .

"You've dreamed. We've felt the prophecy of dreams,"
Said Mmirrimann, voice thundering in silence.
Dread rose like bile into Ssruuanne, her hearts.
She felt the child inside the cavern, saw her hands
Weave light as if the light were more than light
As boundaries between the universes
That could not once be bridged were bridged, and songs
Not of this world were echoed from the past

And future in repeating symphonies.

Her thoughts flowed out of her into the thoughts
Of every dragon there as long necks swayed
In rhythm to the storm her thoughts had made.
A moan rose from the gathered dragons, strong
Enough to tremble rock inside the mountain.
Dismayed, Wwilliama, standing next to where
Old Mmirrimann's eyes whirled emotions dense
With fear into cavern's echoing,
Cried out, "the human girl must die!" as males
Throughout the cavern roared assent and rage
The way Mmlynn had said they would the night
She'd forced Ssruuanne to tell about her dreams.

The girl's blood beat inside Ssruuanne's two hearts.
The girl won't die, she said inside herself.
Her thought had power like the power burned
Into the light that flowed from young girl's hands.
It cut into the rage and silenced it.
The eight old dragons looked at her, eyes shocked.
No one had ever silenced dragon rage,
Not in the history of dragonkind.

"Your foolishness will bring about our doom."
Ssruuanne was shocked to hear her voice ring out.
The voice of prophecy was in her words.
"New days are coming on all dragonkind.
The human girl is part of powers stronger
Than fire and claw. She will not, cannot die!"

The silence was intense, devouring thought.

"The males cannot accept your dreams," Sshruunak,

The leader of the young males boomed into the silence,
His great voice raw and ugly in the cavern.
Black scales shined power from his whirling eyes.
His neck was rigid, challenging Ssruuanne.

"The girl is one of us!" The voice of prophecy
sliced once again through strength and mindless rage.

Sshruunak's great head swayed, fear replacing rage.
He tried to speak, but could not speak, the geas
Of prophecy so powerful it shattered
His will and forced a silence in his hearts.
He forced his legs to move; he bumped against
The male beside him. He moved back, strained toward
The tunnel that would let him find a ledge to leap
Into the air and stretch his reason into wings.

A movement vast as nightmares stirred the conclave,
The dragon society's great unity now chaos.
The tunnels filled with dragons fleeing prophecy
As darkness filled with heatless waves of flame.
Dismay rose up into Ssruuanne and echoed
Into the minds of dragons fleeing her.
She felt the pain of times long past as steel
Brought death past iron-hard scales to dragon flesh.

What was the human girl to her? she cried.
She was a dragon, not the mother of a child.

~ 13 ~

Weaving and Dragon Song

Ruanne sat by the small triangle window,
The morning's light a comfort past the storm.
She pumped the small wood loom and fed the strands
Of hair from mountain goats into the shuttle,
Her hands in constant rhythm as she wove
Each row of heavy cloth into a rug.

She tried to concentrate upon the wisdom
Of Selen who, upon her loom, had woven
A tapestry of man's and woman's flesh
So human love could populate the world.
Thoughts turned to images: Ruarther caught
By madness, storming from her life to wilderness,
Snow fields a glittering in morning light.

A knocking broke into her reverie.
She deftly tied the weaving so the row
Of grey and blue would stay in place for later,
Got up, and greeted Reestor at the door.
The old man looked pale, weary in the light,
Deep eyes ringed dark below white eyebrows, hair.
She smiled and stood aside to let him stomp
Into the cottage, cold around him biting
Into the room warm from the morning fire.

"You're early for your rounds," she said, her sadness

Surprising her inside her too soft voice.

Inside his heavy coat he looked more like
A bear than man, she thought. A wildness clung
To all the men who hunted for the game
That let the village live through winter storms.
She wondered if she ought to leave her cottage
And make the journey to the nearest town.
Ruarther was the one who'd kept her here.
If only he could be the man she loved
And not the man negating who he was.

But now? She smiled as Reestor growled as if
He truly were a bear. He shrugged his coat
Off shoulders strengthened by the years he'd spent
Outdoors before they'd made him village leader.
He walked toward the fire, put out his hands,
Then turned to look into her dark green eyes.

"I saw my father and my brother die," he said.
"I didn't live here then. I moved here later –
When mother couldn't stand the thought of Breenan.

"Two dragons came upon the town all fire.
You seldom saw more than a single dragon then.
We call our fights with them The Dragon War,
But dragons were so powerful they fought
In ones and twos while humans fought with armies.
My father took his great long bow and hit
The older dragon, Pphhitin, in his one good eye.
The younger Mmirrimann went wild,
His breath so hot it fired the town's wood roofs;
His claws sent dozens to their early graves.

"The great green brute not only burned our house,
But Mmirrimann flung down upon my father,
The dragon killer, scorching flesh with fire.
He left Da's body black as smoky quartz,
So burned light seemed translucent through the skull
Left bare without a shred of flesh on bone.
The smell still visits me at night sometimes.
My brother tried to drive a metal spear
In Mmirrimann, but didn't have the strength.
The dragon swatted him away and drove
A broken rib and death into his heart."

Ruanne stood silent, waiting. Reestor looked
At memories he'd long ago suppressed.
He suddenly looked up into her eyes.

"I don't like kings," he said. "The rich men live
Rich lives while those of us who find survival
In places where the rich would never live
Develop bonds much stronger than privation,
But Clayton's Peace has given us good lives.
No human, nor a dragon's died from war
For all the years I've lived since father died."

Ruanne stayed silent, waiting, spirit strung
So taut it seemed as if she ought to scream.

"We see more dragons in the sky each year,"
He said at last. "They have evolved, and we
Are still the humans that we've always been."
He paused and gathered up reluctant thoughts.
"Ruarther's craziness will stir their hearts
And bring about a rage we haven't faced . . ."

Ruanne let out the breath she'd held too long.
She shook her head. "I know," she said. "But what?"
She paused. "The witch's daughter shouldn't die.
The children in the village shouldn't face
The rage of dragon fire and raking claws."

Determined, Reestor looked at her. "You know
The dragon songs," he said. "You've heard them sing
Inside your head. You have to let them know
Ruarther's left our village, lost his mind ..."

"I've never said I hear the songs," Ruanne said softly.
She felt a numbing coldness chilling her.
Not this, she thought. Not this, she pleaded. Please.

"I see it in your eyes, the way you shine inside,"
The old man said. "I've lived too long a life.
I hardly sleep, but still, you're like the witch's child."

His words struck like a blow. She was a witch?

"Ruarther's left me all alone," she said.
"I've loved him since we both were children, babes . . ."

"He's gone, Ruanne. You've got to let him go."

"I've never spoken to a dragon, never . . .
They'll never answer me . . . they'll never hear . . ."

"You've got to try. The children don't deserve
To die because Ruarther caused a war . . ."

Ruanne escaped from Reestor's burning eyes
And looked at where she sat upon the loom.

She shook her head. What could she really do?
She said a silent prayer to sweet Selen.
She'd always forced the dragon's songs away.
She was her mother's child. She'd known the witch,
But never once had felt a bond with her.
How could she speak to dragons when the man
She loved was in the wilderness, his heart
Enraged against a dragon that had spoken to him.

She looked at Reestor, panic in her eyes.
A woman who could talk to dragons brought
A curse upon herself. The villagers would drive
Her from the village, forcing her to live
Away from people that she'd loved since birth.
She'd seen the fate that witches had to face.

She sighed and tried to deny who she was.
She flopped about inside herself, a fish
Caught from a stream and thrown upon the bank.
The village children couldn't die, not if
She had abilities that might protect them.
The old man looked past eyes into her heart.

~ 14 ~

The Substance of Light

The frost upon the window melted. Wei
Stared out at evening skies and watched as
dragons
Launched flight from caves in greater numbers than
She'd ever seen before, their coloured scales
Dramatic in the sunset's pulsing fires.
She wondered what was wrong. They all seemed stressed,
As if they had to flee their underground.
She watched to see the golden dragon's scales,
But if she flew, she flew outside Wei's sight.
She watched until the shadows brought the night,
Then went to sit beside the fireplace fire.

In front of warmth brought by the cheerful flames
She felt half dazed, as if the day's events
Had been too much, and now she wanted rest.
She looked down at her fingers, made a bar
Of light stream out into the darkness, held
It in the air until it looked as if
It were a substance rather than a stream of light.
She smiled, then stopped the motions making light.
The light fell down and dully clinked on stone.

Her mind was suddenly awake; a chill
Made hair behind her neck stand up and crawl.
The bar was fading on the floor, the light
Bleached out, its substance round and strangely long,

As if its substance were not made on earth.

She put her legs beneath her, stretched her hand,
And gingerly, as if it might be hot,
Touched light congealed into a strange, long rod.
The rod was warm and seemed to still contain
A memory of light that it had been.
She sat back, saw the golden dragon's eyes
Stare as it flew so close above her head.
She felt the darkness shift, as if her time
Were not the time where she was sitting by
A fireplace burning warmth into the cottage.

She made another stream of steady light
And welded it into the rod, and then
She made, bemused, another rod until
She had a rabbit cage designed to capture
The meal she had not had for much too long.

She looked toward her mother's empty bed
And saw her mother faintly in the dark.
Behind her mother, coaching her, his hands
So large they seemed as if they had the strength
To hold the world, her father, dead so long
She only had the vaguest memory
Of what his face had looked like during life,
Was pantomiming every move her mother
Was making as she sent hand moves to Wei.

Wei gasped. Her mother looked into her eyes,
Smiled sadly, let the dark intensify,
And left the room to emptiness and night.
Wei felt as if she'd never move again.
She glanced toward the rabbit trap she'd made.

Her mother, from her grave, had made her daughter
As powerful as any witch alive.
She felt the song she'd sing to bring the rabbits
To where they'd find themselves inside her trap.

She felt so restless that she rose and walked
To where the window looked into the night.
Outside she saw the flames of dragon breath
Light up the darkness like the fireflies did
On summer nights. A dragon knew no fear.
Their largeness dwarfed the strength that humans had.
What madness made them fireflies in the dark?

She moved her hands, her eyes intent on where
She'd seen her father's and her mother's forms.
She concentrated on the golden dragon's scales,
Imagined how they'd felt upon its face,
And let her fingers shoot light through the air.
A golden scale, as hard as iron, hung in the air,
Burned with a light so bright it blinded Wei.
She brought the scale onto her arm. Singed flesh,
Strong smells, and pain brought tears into her eyes.
She felt so strange she thought she heard the stars
Sing songs of dragon fire into the night.
Her tingling arm felt like it was not hers,
But separate, more dragon than a human arm.

The light stopped flowing, made her gasp;
She slumped down to the floor, her consciousness
A dream she'd conjured from her mother's grave.

~ 15 ~

The Beginning of War

One

Sshruunak fled high into the winter skies.
He left the conclave as his blood raged fear,
Leaped from the nearest ledge into the air
And blindly flew toward the mountain peaks,
His black wings driven down so fiercely hard
He rose and rose until the air was thinner
Than what his lungs could gulp into his hearts.

His thoughts kept singing, Ssruuanne! Ssruuanne!
The dragon witch! The witch that ruled his tongue!
And made it so he could not think or speak.
He'd felt her power, felt her binding power
Imprison him, a male! Into her will!

At last, his head so light from lack of air
His dizziness leached weakness to his wings,
He wheeled toward the peaks, in moonlight, far
Below him, silver shining light on snow.
He drifted, thoughtless, like a shadow stained
In darkness of the dark beyond the moon,
Then saw, far off, long down the mountain slopes,
A fire built by a human fighting cold.

He did not think, but moved his long, dark wings
And let his rage stoke dragon furnaces.
Humiliation was a fire that death

Would turn to triumph born of dragon power.
He rumbled deep inside his chest and roared!

Two

Ruarther felt as if he'd fought a war.
He looked at Cragdon's haggard face and grimaced.
They'd moved on crusts of hardened snow that caved
Deep holes they had to clamber out of shaking.
They'd laboured upward, slow as creeping turtles,
Until they'd seen the ridge that jutted black
Against the blinding light of sun-struck snow.
Night-cold had burned their faces with its knives
When, at long last, they'd reached the ridge and trees.
The weariness they felt was like a weight
That would not let them move their arms or legs.

When Cragdon saw the distant puffs of flame
That flickered all along the mountain's slopes,
He barely motioned as he pointed at the lights.

"What's that?" he croaked, his weary voice half dead.

Ruarther forced himself to stand and stare.
He listened to the wilderness's silence,
Felt strangeness make him grab his bow and crouch,
His eyes a restlessness scanned at the sky.

"Your bow!" he hissed at Cragdon. "Hurry! Now!"

He saw the dragon as it flew at them,
Its blackness huge inside the moon's bright light.
He notched his arrow at the hurtling blackness
As Cragdon, suddenly aware of death's

Black dragon hide, let go another arrow.
The dragon roared, its roar so threatening and loud
It made Ruarther tremble from its rage.
He turned and saw the space between the boulders.

"Behind the stones!" he yelled. "Our war has come!"

Three

An arrow skipped a half-inch from his eyes
Off scales into the dark, but then another
Burned into his right eye's pupil, sending
Small streams of blood and pain into the wind.
He roared his rage and pain and soared as ground
Brushed hard and cold against the tip of wings.
He hated humans! Death! he raged. Death! Death!
He wheeled toward the puny men again
And roared as if his voice were dredged from realms
Where humans congregated past their graves
In lands of nothingness and cold despair.

Four

He would not be afraid again, Ruarther swore
Beneath his breath behind the boulder's shield.
He glanced at Cragdon, saw the dragon's breath
Had seared the bobcat coat he wore, exposing flesh.
The campfire burned its cheer into the night.

He heard the dragon turn. He waited, breath
Forgotten as he tried to time his move
So that his strength could send a deadly arrow
Into the dragon's eye and make it flee.

The dragon's wings were loud. Ruarther moved
Into the open, saw an arrow buried
Inside the dragon's right eye, drew his bow,
And tried to drive another arrowhead
Into the same eye spewing dragon blood.
The dragon's flame enveloped him with agony.
He could not hear nor see the dragon rake
Its legs into the surface of the snow
Or see a second arrow's shaft protruding
Out from the dragon's eye, blood staining snow,
A waterfall of blood that fell to earth.

Five

Sshruunak's pain flared as if the universe
Had disappeared into a blood-red fire.
He felt wings drive into the freezing snow.
He barely lifted from the ground and death.
His claws extended, pain a reddish haze,
He tried to rake the flesh he'd burned with fire.
But dragon will was not enough to let him wheel
To swoop toward the humans yet again.
I've damaged both my wings, he thought. Both wings!

Instead of breathing fire at enemies
He flew toward the caves and thought about
The words Ssruuanne had used to silence him:
"The girl is one of us," she'd said. The prophecy
A geas that led him, in his foolishness,
To court his death confronting puny men.

~ 16 ~

Ending Dragon Community

Inside the conclave's cavern elders sat
Upon the great, stone ledge, their eyes so bright
The darkness near them whorled with coloured
   lights.
Ssruuanne, her spirit broken by the chaos
Of dragons violating rules set down
To let community replace the greed
And singularity of dragonkind,
Joined song with Mmirrimann as elders strove
To calm the storm as dragons fled from caves
Into the bitter cold of winter skies.

Wwilliama, feeling that her words had caused
The chaos when she'd let her fear of humans
Subdue her sentience, worked hard to meld
Her spirit's song to all the others' songs,
The elder's unity the sanity
That could undo the madness firing hearts
With vengeance borne on frantic dragon wings.

At last they found Sshruunak's black rage, the fear
Inside his hearts so dark it made him blind.
They felt him hurtling toward two humans
Beside a fire that burned against the cold.
Ssruuanne sent songs of peace and calm through skies
To where his fearsome rage was uncontrolled.
The elder song inside the cavern rose

Into a symphony of power filled
With whirling eyes and hearts that tried to mend
The great black dragon's rage and mindless fear.
The cavern echoed with the voices drawn
From dragon chests and massive vocal cords.

They felt the violation of the truce
Made with the human Clayton, King of Tryon.
They felt the arrow burn into Sshruunak's dark eye
And felt the burning agony of human skin
Seared by the fire of dragon breath and rage.
Their song intensified past who they were.
Sshruunak turned, hurtled at the human flesh
Until a hunter jumped from hiding:
Another arrow: Burning agony.
Flames wrapped the hunter in its searing shroud,
His pain, Sshruunak's pain echoing a war
Into the cavern, counterpoint to calm
The elders had been sending out through skies.

The elders' wings flared out and made a wind
Inside the cavern, sweeping out through tunnels.
The males, spread out along the mountains' slopes,
Sensed pain enveloping Sshruunak, felt wind
Inside the tunnels and the safe, dark caves.
They felt the desperation in the elders
That tried to calm the rage that filled night skies.
Sshruunak fled humans and their deadly arrows;
The conclave elders strove to turn to order,
To end the stirring of a world enraged.

"The peace is done," said Mmirrimann. "The dragons
And humans know the taste of blood again."
His words destroyed the elders' song and plunged

The cavern deep in dark intense enough
To spread across the winter of the earth.

Ssruuanne slumped on the eldest dais.
Inside the darkness of her spirit, small,
She felt the witch's child and saw her hands
Create a golden dragon's scale and brand
It deep in flesh, transforming human flesh.
A scale not human in a human's flesh!

Before the peace all dragonkind had faced
Eventual decline into extinction.
The endless wars had slowly whittled down
The dragon numbers, one great spirit dying
And then another, slowly decimating
A race that humans always had outbred.

The young males thought that dragonkind could win
Against the tides of human machinations.
They knew their strength and did not understand
That war was more than strength or dragon will.
Sshruunak had breached the truce, and now? She
	shuddered.

The image of the human armies mustered
Against the dragons while the last war raged
Swam through her memories, the smell of flesh
Left rotting in the fields as dragons died,
Their power little use against the tactics
King Clayton used to slowly decimate
The warriors with their dragon hides evolved
To keep a dragon's spirit from an arrow's flight.
She heard, inside her head, the mourning chants
As dragon warrior after dragon warrior died.

"What now?" she asked as Mmirrimann stared blankly
At cavern darkness. "Wisdom still exists."

"The witch's child is dead," the dragon mourned.
"I felt your vision, saw the withering
If rage was loosed into the world again.
Sshruunak's a hero now inside the caves.
He'll want revenge against the girl, her death."

Wwilliama said, "This will not be. I caused
This madness with a mindless spew of words.
The males will listen. I can see my madness,
They've got capacity to see their madness too."

The geas came on Ssruuanne and made her cry,
"The girl is still alive! She'll stay alive!
I'll use my dragon life to find the peace!"

Old Mmirrimann looked at his ancient lover,
Then slowly dragged himself into the dark.

~ 17 ~

Separation in the Wilderness

His stupefaction, as he sat in snow
    Beside the boulder as his pain seared skin,
    Kept him from seeing Cragdon packing up
To struggle back the way they'd come across
The treachery of fields of blinding snow.

"I'm leaving now," the young man said, his face
A mask of pain where dragon's fire had burned
His arm and side. "I'm done. I'm going home."

Ruarther, from his seat, looked up and stared
Into the young man's bleary-looking eyes.

"You've lost your mind," he said. "We're injured, bad.
Until we've got our hurts controlled, the village
Is just a dream you'll never reach alive."

The pre-dawn cold was hinting at the light
Now filtering along the eastern ridges.

"I knew I'd have to go alone," the young man said.
"You're crazy. Why I followed you out here
Is something that I'll never understand.
I didn't realise we'd start a war."

"The witch's child has stirred the dragons up,"
Ruarther growled. "You're suffering from burns

Inflicted by a dragon hurtling from the skies.
It had no reason to attack our camp."

"Perhaps it read our minds and gave us warning
That murdering a child is not the way
To keep the human/dragon peace," he said.
He felt as if he'd shrugged away a shroud
And straightened out his head, his muddled thinking.
"I'll send the hunters out with fresh supplies.
You'll have to keep alive until you're found."

Ruarther looked inside the rage that boiled
So deep it was the substance of his life.
He growled again, but did not say a word.

As Cragdon looked at him, the man he'd seen
As better than a man could ever be,
His hero since he'd been a child who'd hung
Upon the village's stone walls to watch
For hunters coming from the woods with game
On tripods made of fresh-cut branches roped
Around their hips, or slung on massive shoulders,
He wondered why he'd failed to see the truth.
The grim, dark man who leaned against the boulder
Was not a village man, but bound in spirit
To raving spirit beasts whose sentience
Danced chaos born from rage into the world.
He'd learned that as they'd struggled through the snow.

He shook his head and looked toward the slopes
That angled down toward the only place
He really cared about inside the world.
He tried to conjure up his wife and child
So that they'd know he'd left his craziness

And started travelling back to those he loved.
He'd heard his wife's scared cry and walked away
To follow where Ruarther's madness led.
But all he saw was anguish in the fields
Of snow he'd have to cross to find the village.

"I'm going now," he said. The snow shined brightly
As sunrise danced with sky fire as it crept
Across the treacherous, white miles of crust.
He wondered if he had the strength to make
It to his family, the life he loved.
He briefly wondered where the dragon was.
It too was facing weeks of burning pain.
He'd seen the arrows lodged inside its eye.
Blood spilled was still stained on the campsite's snow.
He shook his head, then moved out from the ridge.

Ruarther failed to hear, or see, when Cragdon
Began his journey home. He fought to block
His pain from consciousness and tried to focus
Upon the task of finding peace again
By murdering the witch's child and letting dragons
Go back to living in their caves away
From hunters and their villages and homes.
He tried to see the child's unnatural eyes
And wondered how a witch with minor skills
Could birth a witch so powerful her strings
Turned dragons into puppets of her will.

He felt the golden dragon's whirling eyes
Confront him, heard the power in her voice,
But when he looked around to see her body,
The wilderness and sky were empty, fevers
Unquenchable inside his raw, red flesh.

The fever that he'd faced inside the village
Was nothing next to what was burning in him now.
He cupped snow in his hands and spread its cold
Upon his burns and coughed inside his lungs.
He wondered if he'd be alive when dawn
Lit up the sky again and wheeled another day.

But then he knew: He'd kill the witch's child.
He'd give Ruanne the peace his love deserved.
When he'd brought peace, she'd see the man he was.
He'd let the dragons settle back into their lives.

He forced himself onto his feet and put
More wood to burn upon the dying fire.

~ 18 ~

The Meeting of Wei and Ssruuanne

One

Inside her dream Wei flew through skies so blue
They seemed to vibrate with a pulsing life –
And then she was awake, the fire stoked down,
Air frigid, dark intense, more night than night.
Her mother, gleaming, sat upon her bed
And seemed to look at worlds Wei could not see.
Wei huddled in the covers, warm, content
To see her mother in her life again.
She did not feel the weirdness that she'd felt
When she had seen her mother's form before.
But then her mother sensed she was awake
And stood, light streaming from her sudden movement.
She did not speak, but stared with sightless eyes.
Behind her mother in the faint blue haze,
Vague, other figures huddled, eyes unfocused.

Wei carefully sat up, the covers clutched
Beneath her chin, her heartbeats in her ears.
Her mother waved her arm. The room's deep cold
Seemed colder still. Wei stared, afraid.
Each time she'd seen her mother in the room
She'd not felt fear, but now a warmth spread over
Her trembling body, banishing the cold,
And in the warmth she felt as if she'd lost
The little girl she was and found a self
Not made at birth, but forged from hands that waved

A spectral light into the night's cold dark.
She felt as if she tottered on a cliff
Above a canyon plunging down sheer walls
Toward the River Lethe[3] far below.
Entranced, she slid from covers, stood up straight,
Heart larger than her heart had ever been.

Two

While moving from the conclave cavern out
Into the tunnel leading to her cave,
Ssruuanne felt warmth beneath her scales, a strangeness.
She stopped and felt the geas come over her,
This time so powerful it seemed to seize
Control of who she was. What now? she asked,
Her two hearts struggling against the power
That flooded deep into her brain and made
Her want to leap into the air and fly toward
The human girl's small cottage in the dark.

She felt the witch inside the tunnel with her.
Impossible, she thought, the dead did not
Walk down a corridor where dragons lived.
The dead were veiled from her reality.
In irritation at the urgency
She felt, she forced her legs to root themselves
Into the tunnel's floor, her exercise
Of dragon will a force against the geas.

The dragon race was fading everywhere,
But here inside the mountain, where the peace
They'd forged had held four dozen years and let
Them build community now threatened by
Sshruunak's rage brought about by how the geas

Had shot into the conclave's fear, they'd thrived.
What madness shattered through a dragon's will?

Sshruunak's black rage had violated peace.
The dragons' center was disintegrating,
The evolution that had caused a burst
Of eggs and dragonets now close to failing.
Her dreams had let her know the precipice
Above the edge's void they tottered on.
She felt the sadness dragging Mmirrimann
Back to his cave, the sense he felt at having
His greatest triumphs turn to bitter ash.

He'd made the peace, his will implacable
Against both dragon solitude and rage
And humans raised to hate and fear all dragons.
He'd found a way to build community
In spite of dragon patterns forged through time,
But now her dreams had shaken what he'd built
And freed the demons dragon spirits spawned
And set to raging as extinction wrapped
A suffocating web around their race
And threatened ending all of dragonkind.

What should she do? She asked herself. The geas
Was like a cloud that danced with lightning bolts,
So powerful it took away her strength.
She was no human who the spirit world
Could enter, forcing her to do its will.
She did not have to fly to find the girl.

At last she sighed. She walked toward the ledge.

Three

Unwilling, Wei walked haltingly toward
The cottage door. She was not dressed for cold,
But as her mother moved her spectral arms
And light danced in the darkness, warmth surrounded
Her body, forced the winter cold away.
Beside the door she glanced back at her mother.
Her father, fainter than her mother's form,
Stood just behind the light her mother cast,
The love the two of them had felt in life
Now emanating out toward their daughter.
Without a thought she opened up the door
And walked onto the path she'd made with light
Into the drifts of snow and looked toward
The mountains, winter's black and bitter skies.
She felt the dragon even though she felt
Half blind inside the swirling, freezing dark.
She strained to see it as its wings beat air.

Four

The Old One sent a stream of steady flame
To clear a circle by the human girl,
The snow evaporating in a cloud of steam,
And flared her golden wings and touched the ground.
She felt the changing of the world she'd known,
The keening of a dragon as they'd fought for life
Against a horde of tiny men that shot
Their arrows further than they'd ever shot –
Their triumph singing songs of dragon death.
She felt the girl's bright eyes, as calm as water
On pools without a breath of wind, sweep over
Her, soaking up her spirit, seeing past

Her scales into the beating of her hearts.

"You're Wei," she said, her voice surprising her.
The girl kept staring, drawing strength and power
From where her mother stood beside her bed.

"Ssruuanne," the young girl said, "your name's Ssruuanne."
She sounded awed, as if she could not grasp
That she was standing in the winter snow
Without a coat or boots and hearing words
Said by a dragon only seen in skies.

The geas collapsed. Ssruuanne felt free, but stood
Her ground. What did the young girl want? What caused
Her mother's spirit's restlessness and power?

Five

Wei did not move, but stared, eyes soaking
Ssruuanne into her memories and self.
The golden scale she'd burned into her arm
Pulsed hot and made her feel her blood spin back
Into a time when humans' ancient power
Flowed through their flesh, their minds, their deepest selves.

Six

The girl's eyes stopped their searching, glanced at ground.
Ssruuanne looked at the girl and saw the dragon
Inside the storm of spirits in her spirit.
There's something new upon the earth, she thought,
And with the thought she seemed to hear a chant
That flooded her with hope and dreams and love.
She snorted, shook seduction from the chant

And looked toward the tiny human girl
So frail before her dragon massiveness.

Fear coursed into her blood and made her feel
As if the human girl were part of her,
As if the penetrating eyes saw cells
Inside her body like they saw her scales.
She tore her eyes away from Wei and looked
Toward where dawn was brewing early day.
She spread her wings and lifted from the ground.
The girl's intensity intruded on her self
In ways impossible to understand.

~ 19 ~

Touching a Dragon's Mind

Inside her room, Ruanne sat still beside
Her loom and rocked the rocking chair so slightly
It hardly seemed to move. Old Broar and Reestor
Sat near her, waiting, nervousness at weirdness
Inside their eyes and drawn, pale, frightened faces.
Ruanne let thoughts drift outward, fleeing light
Toward the mountains rising in the west.

Old Broar had come that morning, shook his bones,
And told her that she had to let her heritage
Unlock the possibilities of peace.
She'd shook her head, still terrified of how
The villagers would act to find a witch
Inside the woman that they'd always known,
But then gave in, her stress so great she felt
As if she couldn't take another breath.

The only time she'd let her thoughts drift west
Was when she'd been distracted or was close
To sleep and in-between awake and sleep.
For years she'd forced her mind to shy away
From songs vibrating deep inside her bones.
She'd always known the songs were dragon songs,
But lied and told herself she heard no songs.

As morning light intensified and spread
Across her flagstone floor, she saw Crayllon,

The witch, stare at the villagers as one,
And then another, picked up heavy stones
And threw them at her and her tiny child.
The child, too young to understand, screamed, frightened,
Her body shaking as her mother stood
And glared at men and women taunting her,
Their faces red and ugly in the morning light.

Crayllon had stood her ground, dishevelled, rage
Distorting who she was, and held the girl
Behind her plain black skirts as she was hit
And bloodied on her arm and then her face.
Her husband newly dead, she stood accused
Of killing him, a man she'd always loved.

She'd stood as silent as the stones that bruised
Her flesh and spirit cut her off from people
She'd lived with all her life. Her witchery,
Inherited from parents who'd helped to end
The wars for Clayton through their dragon-talking,
Transmuted from a force that ended war
Into a twisted evil filled with death.

Grim words had sealed her fate through innuendo.
This even though her husband's wounds had come
From dire wolves chanced upon while hunting goats
When he had climbed too far into the mountains.

He was too strong to die, his kin had said,
Their grief as bitter as their lives had been.
His wife had caused his death. She was a witch.
He'd faced the wolves a dozen times and lived.
Why had he died this time and not before?
She had to die, and so they'd used their tongues

To brew a storm that led to men with stones
Hurled with excitement at a woman, child,
Themselves, their fears, the village's ruined heart.

The woman stood as blood poured down her face.
Her hair was matted with her sticky blood.
She turned and walked toward the dragon caves,
Her body shielding her child, as taunts
Of villagers pursued her as she fled.
Somehow she'd kept the stones from striking Wei,
The tiny child filled with a mindless terror.

Inside her trance Ruanne lost where she was.
Her vision burned into her young child's mind.
She'd seen distorted rage and mocking voices
From where she'd stood beside her mother watching
The ugliness outside their house's windows.

She'd never be a witch, she'd thought. Not her.
She'd be a village woman safe from stones.
She knew her mother knew the art of talking
To dragons even though she kept it silent.
She knew that if she tried she'd hear a voice
Inside her mind where only she could hear.

Old Broar had been the one that stopped the madness.
He'd stepped between the witch and sneering men
And women throwing stones and screeching curses
And made them hesitate and told the witch
To leave, to save her child, to keep the village
From doing what would stain its spirit dark.
And somehow, standing there, he'd backed the men
And women spreading lies into retreat
And let Crayllon flee to the mountain peaks.

She startled in the rocking chair. Chills ran
Along her arms and made her want to flee
Away from chaos pounding in her head.
The dragon song she'd felt before had throbbed
With harmonies that shimmered, danced in air.
Fear, rage, regret, intensity, confusion,
Cold calculation, desperation stopped
Her rocking, made her rigid as a spire
Of stone shot up into a storming sky.
She felt as if she'd travelled endless miles
As dreams half-formed inside her mind, then faded.

Old Broar and Reestor felt the storm she faced
And blanched, their fears alive inside of them.
Their bodies made them want to get up, flee
Into the wilderness away from what
Was pummelling Ruanne with churning visions.
Contortions marred the beauty in her face.
She looked as if she'd fallen in a pit of fear.
They had to reach into their deepest selves
To sit and watch their young friend face her storm.

An ancient spirit felt Ruanne and stared
Into a human that she'd never thought would brave
Immensities inside a dragon's mind.
Mmlynn had heard the tales of human speech
Inside a dragon's mind, but had not thought
That she would ever feel it in her head.
She knew her mother heard the thoughts of humans,
But then her mother was more than a dragon . . .
Ruanne felt fear rise up as if a stream
Had overflowed its banks and swept all life
Before it as it tore apart the earth.
The dragon seized control of who she was.

She forced herself to calm. She said, inside
Herself, "We do not want another war."

And then Ruanne saw where a long, dark ridge
Rose out of endless fields of drifted snow.
Ruarther sat beside a campfire, face
So hideous with burns from dragon fire
She cried out in the silent room and made
The two men get up from their chairs, their hearts
Contesting wills to keep them in the cottage.

The dragon seemed surprised to see the vision,
But then its calm washed through Ruanne and let
Her feel herself again. She looked at Reestor,
Despair at what she'd seen so strong and urgent
She dropped the dragon song and felt a panic
That seemed to make her life irrelevant.
Her eyes were raw with tears streaked down her cheeks.

"Ruarther's burned by dragon fire," she said.
"The war's begun. He made the war he wanted,
And soon its fires will sweep out of the caves."

Old Broar looked, frightened, at her eyes and forced
Himself to smile. "You touched a dragon's mind,"
He said. "You didn't die. We have a way
Of telling them we do not want more war."

Grim, Reestor moved and took Ruanne into his arms.
In spite of how he felt he understood
The panicked feeling pummelling Ruanne.
Ruarther was a quandary escaped
From what a normal human ought to be.

"We'll find him. He won't die out there," he said.

Ruanne's eyes filled with tears. "I love him. Damned,"
She said. "I love him even though he's crazy,
Concocting senselessness endangering
The people that he thinks his deeds protects."

Outside the children started shouting, laughing
As morning started up life's old routines.

~ 20 ~

Brewing Dragon War

Inside his cave Sshruunak's dark thoughts unleashed
A constant rage that blistered him with lightning
That made him thrash and slam into the darkness
Of stone. It made him feel a sharp, clean pain.
He felt a fire so fierce it made scales burn
Into his flesh and scar his spirit's song.

He'd let the healers come, extract the arrows,
And wrap his bloody eye with salve and webbing
Designed to let a membrane heal the wound,
But then he'd sent long streams of dragon fire
To singe the other males brave enough
To bring their fury to his cold, dark lair.
He brooded in the darkness like the worm
The humans once had said described his kind.
He'd always thought himself impervious
To any human wiles and could not understand
How two small humans had defeated him.

When old Wwilliama came and stood outside
His cave and called to him, he snorted fire
And rumbled with his incoherent rage,
But chasing elders off was not as easy
As threatening the friends he'd had since birthing.
The old, dark dragon waited for his fire
To spend its breath, then came inside, her eyes
So wild with whirling colours that she seemed

As potent as Ssruuanne upon the dais.
She stood in light made by her eyes and curled
Her lips so that her rows of teeth gleamed white
Inside the storm of hatred that he'd brewed.

"You're hiding from yourself," she said, her voice
A whipping blade of anger. "Now you know
Why peace was made before all dragonkind
Was lost to history and ancient myths."

Sshruunak let silence stretch and coil its menace
Into discomfort as the elder stood
And stared implacably at where his eye
Was blind, her stance aggressive, challenging.

"This universe cannot let dragons live
While humans breed like rabbits in the spring,"
He growled at last. "We live; they die, or else
They live, and we become an ancient myth.
You used the words; I spit them in your craw!"

Wwilliama's eyes grew more intense. She snorted,
A puff of fire flared out to light the cave.

"I was a fool," she said. "I heard the geas Ssruuanne
Called from the ancient spirits of our race
And let my hatred of the humans crush
My sentience and send you out to where
You were as big a fool as me when I
Called down destruction on the human girl.

"When Mmirrimann negotiated peace
I thought he was insane, but we are thriving
Inside these caves. Our numbers used to fall

Year after year through centuries of time.
There's dragons birthed from eggs each week inside
The birthing caves right now. Extinction's not
The danger that it was a hundred years ago.
The peace has got to hold. It's got to hold."

He stirred. "The young will follow me," he said.
"I've heard their talk outside the cave for days."

"You think you are a leader then?" she asked.
"Like Mmirrimann? Ssruuanne? The ones who made
It possible for us to live our lives
Without the threat of arrows in our eyes?"

The blackness in him stirred alive a force
More powerful than any dragon was.
It overwhelmed his pain and blindness, swept
Aside the reason in Wwilliama's voice,
And roared into the cave so loud the stones
Above their heads began to tremble, crack.

Inside the universe of sound Wwilliama
Stood still, despair a wailing in her head
That echoed back into the times when dragons
Were solitary in their greediness.
Inside the cave Sshruunak seemed like a nightmare,
Wings black, his spirit black as shining wings.
She stared into the storm of who he was
And tried to find his sentience, the key
That could unlock the future of their kind
And let them all avoid a dragon war
Where young fought elders as their futures waned
Into a memory that few would know.

"You cannot kill the human girl," she said.
"Ssruuanne is eldest. She has seen the song
That's gathering inside our dragon hearts."

The silence was so sudden that it echoed.
He glared at her, his eye so fierce it seemed
As if it had the will to hypnotize all time.

"The humans who were brave enough to send
Their arrows in my eye are dead," he said.
"A single dragon's not the force that dragons
Assembled like a human army are.
Ssruuanne's geas took away my dragonness
And made me silent when I meant to speak.
The girl's as dead as those two hunters are."

"Ssruuanne and Mmirrimann will fight against
Your craziness," Wwilliama said. "The elders
Won't easily forsake the future of our race."

"The elders battling the young?" he sneered.
His blackness seemed to stretch outside the cave
Into the winter cold and coal-black night.
"The young will win," he said. "The young will win."

"We'll see," Wwilliama answered, sadness like
A pool of water covering her spirit.
"We'll see what dawn and dragon hearts will bring."

She turned and left the cave. Sshruunak saw deep
Into the universe and saw the power
Of rage engulfing all the earth in flame.
He was a dragon like the beasts who'd ruled
The earth before the humans found the tools

They'd used to fight against a dragon's strength.

"The hunters and the girl are dead," he said.
"And if the elders have to die, they'll die."

Ssruuanne would never use her geas on him.
She'd used it once, but never would again.
Inside the darkness of his cave he saw
His blackness leading as a hundred dragons
Flew massed toward a village wrapped in peace.

~ 21 ~

Inside a Furnace

He felt as if he were inside a furnace,
    The brick kiln burning with a glowing heat,
    His skin so sensitive it seared with pain,
As if he'd touched a fiery red-hot coal
And spread its agony across his face,
Hours blistering into eternity,[4]
The fire from dragon's breath a shroud he wore
That made each wracking gasp for air his life.

Inside this pain he still got to his feet
And gathered wood and kept the fire alive
As night turned day turned night turned day again.
He would not die, he said inside his mind.
He could not think, but still, he told himself.
I will not die. I'll live another day.

A dawn rose golden over mountain peaks.
Snow sheened sky-gold across the wilderness.
Asleep at last, arms twitching uncontrollably
As nightmares danced with fire and pain,
Ruarther did not see the bear rise spectral
From ashes of the dwindling fire so huge
It seemed as if it were the spawn of dragons,
Dark, ragged fur tinged gold by morning light.
Its smell was strong enough to have a whiff
Of sulphur as it shimmered, then solidified
Above the man who whimpered in his sleep.

The great bear wove its arms above the man.
Ruarther woke, his bloodshot eyes afraid.
The bear stood silent, waiting, coiled intensity.
Ruarther tried to gather thoughts from pain,
The shroud of heat consuming who he was.

"I have to kill the witch's child," he croaked,
His throat so dry with heat it hurt to talk.

The bear's eyes gleamed and glared at him.
"Blood is a juice of rarest quality,"[5] it said.

"You are a spirit bear," Ruarther said.
"You have the strength to take this pain away."

The bear just stared at him. Light streamed around
Its massive form and shimmered as the sun
Rose up above the mountain peaks and golden light
Blurred deep into the blue of winter sky.

"I'll feed upon your pain," the great bear said.
"I'll feed upon the pain your hatred burns
Into the human and the dragon worlds."

The fire behind it blazed a dance of flames.
The great bear turned and seemed to sway with winds
Not felt within Ruarther's winter world.
It roared, the sound so loud it shook a crest
Of snow and sent it plummeting from off
The ridge above Ruarther's camp, a cloud
That stung Ruarther's skin and chilled the shroud
Wrapped round his burning flesh and mind.

Ruarther gasped. He could not breathe. The cold

Of nothingness pierced ice into his bones.
He felt as if he had no eyes or ears,
As if his human senses had dissolved
Into a void where men did not belong.

The bear was in the void, a monstrous shape
That had no form, but whirled into a wind
That was no wind, but ash that heaped its blackness
Into a glittering beside a fire
That wisped with smoke into the freezing skies.

Ruarther's lungs gasped air. He shuddered, gulped
The bitter cold into his lungs as if
It were ambrosia, life, unexpected joy!
He was amazed to feel that he was still
Alive, a human not possessed by spirits
That roamed the earth in search of human souls.
He knew the tales. He'd heard them all his life.

He touched his arm. His flesh was hot.
He flinched to feel the pain his touch could cause.
His weariness ached deep inside his mind
And made each joint and bone seem brittle, sore.
He felt the cold. The shroud of fiery heat
Had dissipated when the bear turned back
Into the ash he'd risen from to life.

What now? He asked himself. He was alone.
The fields of snow were blinding bright with sun.
He had to have a fire to stay alive.
The huge, black dragon dove out of the dark
Toward the boulder that he hid behind.
He closed his eyes and felt the wind of wings
That sifted blackness through the moonlit skies.

He had to end the dragon threat of war.
Inside his universe of pain he'd kept that chant.
He glanced toward his bow and deadly arrows.

The bear had given back his life and will.
He'd kill the witch's child. He'd kill the child.
He smiled. He'd rest. Then, with the coming dawn,
He'd start the journey to the plateau where
A cottage sat below the caves of dragons.
He'd drive an arrow through the child's black heart.

~ 22 ~

Journeying to Chaos: Search for Survival

Inside his cave, his massive spirit brooding,
The great male Mmirrimann was still, his hearts'
Swift rhythms slowed to somnolence, near death.
He journeyed through the layers of his self
Inside a mind that knew no boundaries.
The memories ancestors had bestowed
Kaleidoscopic, images swirled ceaselessly
Behind his eyes, summarising history.
The dragon race devolved into a rage
Red-eyed, incensed that human brains could scurry
In bodies small as ants and still wrap them
With ropes that would not let him save themselves.
And still he journeyed through his dragonness
Until he passed the vestiges of what
A dragon was and let the darkness swell
Into a universe much greater than his self.

Mmlynn had told him of the human's words.
She still seemed shaken by the woman's voice.
They did not want a war, but in Sshruunak
War seethed toward a moment when its hate
Would bathe the earth with human/dragon blood
And start the leeching of the dragon race
Toward its final end the way it had
For all the years he'd lived before the peace.
He could not stop Sshruunak without a war.

The young believed he had a hero's hearts
And would not hear as Mmirrimann spoke truth.
They'd fight to keep their dreams of glory come
Again into a world too commonplace.

He told himself that in his memories
Of dragon lives that stretched back centuries
He'd find an answer, find the key to stop
The ancient dragon rage that sapped the strength
They needed if they'd see the birthing caves
Allow the dragonets to grow into day's light.

At last, inside miasma, hearts still slow,
He came into a barren field, a place
Between the stars where sunlight never shined,
Not earth, not space, a place devoid of substance,
Yet real, where shades gloamed in the dusk
And chaos sang into the birth of stars.

He felt the living substances of spirits:
Great animals whose strength had let them flee
Finality of death, the human shades
That teemed and swirled in clouds of mourning, searching
For absolution from the dark that came
Out of their lives and sense of what they'd been,
The dragons flying rage into the dark
Grown monstrous with unwillingness to die
Though some had lived three hundred years or more.

Inside cacophonies' churn Mmirrimann
Searched for an answer to his endless quest
To find a corridor where dragons lived
And did not spiral to their race's death,
But everywhere he looked the universe

Of death whirled clouds of beasts and humans, dragons
That flew at him, their momentary faces
Alive with being, then a trail of mist.
As bright eyes disappeared into the rising
Of other beings with their faces solid,
Then mist, the chaos eddied endlessly.

There was no ending, no beginning, just
A swirling where a train of beings rose
Into their sense of self, then lost themselves
As time coagulated, formed, then flowed
Into the swirl of being, nothingness.
There was a dragon race; there was no race,
Its rising swallowed by the human song
That dominated all the earth; then, like
The dragons, humans were miasma
As planets swung around their suns, and suns
Flared light into their darkness as their fires
Exploded into nova gravities
That swallowed matter near in time and space.

Life swirled into the chaos like the dragons,
The humans, the spirit beasts, the beings found
On other worlds in other times, miasma
Creating, shaping, then destroying as
Forever spun the endless minds of God.

The swirling tugged at Mmirrimann and tried
To suck him deep into its endless maw.
He felt his mind and body disappearing
As dragon after dragon formed, then misted,
Their substance real, then disappeared, time filled
With lives that were, but never were, that sang
And then became a hurricane of souls.

They had no individual substance, life,
But were the matter of the universe.

He fought the tugging, talonned deep the spark
That made him what he was, a dragon great
Enough to brave the journey past his self,
And searched in desperation for a hold
That he could grasp inside the maelstrom's swirl.
At last he saw a single buzz of light
That did not waver, but was fixed inside
The endless swirling, weaving strands of time.
He fought toward the light, the ledge where he
Could spread his wings and launch back to his life.

Time roared with silence, buffeting against
His will, his self, his sense of what he was.
He fought toward the buzz of light and forced
Himself to know himself, his dragon hearts –

And then he saw inside the light a human,
A woman from his place and time now dead,
Surrounded by a knot of humans waving
Their arms, creating substance from the chaos.
They'd forced a bridge between his world and where
He was inside the wind that was no wind.
A golden dragon wavered at the edge
Of where the human spectres generated
The ordered light, the only dragon real
Inside the chaos of the roiling darkness.

He did not know if dragons lived or died
As time swirled from chaotic winds and gloam.
He could not see the corridor he sought
So that Sshruunak's rage would not lead to death

For dragons borning future generations.

He urged himself toward the light and blinked.
He felt his cave's stone walls, hearts quickening,
The chaos just a song inside his ears.

~ 23 ~

Reordering Salvation

One

Ruanne packed carefully, then heaved a sigh.
The hunters would not willingly allow
Her presence as they braved the treachery
Of miles of snow now frozen on its surface.
They'd think she'd be a burden as they watched
For warring dragons and the wounded men,
But she was going if she had to travel
Behind them as they tried to find Ruarther
And Cragdon struggling back to where the village,
Tense, fearful, waited for a dreaded future.
She loved Ruarther even as he caused
The chaos threatening all that she loved.

Outside her cottage Reestor waited, looking
Exhausted, circles black beneath his eyes.
He shook his head to see the pack she'd packed.

"I knew you'd try to go," he said. "A-Brimm
Will try to stop you, but he'll not succeed."
He sighed, his worry, sadness in his eyes.

Ruanne smiled at the village leader, shook
Her head, but silently walked past to where
The hunters gathered as the morning sun
Threw blue, long shadows out from trees.

A-Brimm looked carefully at her and Reestor
The moment that they left her cottage door.
He'd volunteered to lead the search since Cragdon
Was kin, his sister's youngest child, a boy
He'd always liked and thought would be a man
That other men would one day come to value.

Ruanne ignored his eyes, but looked toward
The trail they'd travel as they made their way
Into the slopes and fields that rose snow-bound
Into the mountains where the dragons lived.

When Reestor opened up the wooden gate
The grim-faced hunter shook his head and frowned.

"This trip is not a woman's trip," he said.
"I'll not be blamed for leading you to harm."

Ruanne glanced at his glare, then walked on past
And started down the trail toward the fields
Beyond the denseness of the forest's trees.

A-Brimm turned, desperate, to Reestor, pointed
Toward Ruanne, frustration in the way he stood.

"You're leader. Make her stop," he said. "Who knows
What nightmares that we'll face outside of here."

"Ruarther's hurt and dying," Reestor said.
"We need her here if we can stop this war
Before it overwhelms us all, but I
Can't stop her, so you'll have to keep her safe."

The seven other hunters mumbled, growled

To hear the village leader's words. A-Brimm
Just stared at him, then grabbed his bow and pack
From snow and stalked to where Ruanne had walked.
The other hunters, voices cursing, scrambled
Into the trail Ruanne and he had left.

Two

Blind, stumbling, Cragdon felt his death
Beside him in the snow he'd walked for days.
His body jarred each time he forced his way
Through snow drifts high enough to daunt a man
Who still had youth and endless stores of strength.
Still young, he'd lost both youth and strength to snow.
He forced his muscles through another step,
Another mile, his eyesight blurring, fading
As winter sunlight glared light into eyes.

He'd lost the reason why he kept his legs
Alive with shuffling through the emptiness.
His thoughts were haunted by a dragon's rage
That flamed out from the fullness of a moon
With searing tongues of fire that made his flesh
Smell charred and sweet with putrefaction's rot.
He kept on swatting at the empty air
And flinching as the flames shot out at him.
He thought he'd welcome death when movement
Became too difficult, and life gave out.
He thought he'd smile and take death's hand in his
And feel relief that he, at last, was done.
He could not bring his wife or child alive
Inside his mind. It troubled him, but still . . .

Three

Ruanne walked from the woods into the fields
And squinted at the brightness of the snow.
A-Brimm, ten steps behind, stopped when she stopped.
Behind them hunters started leaving woods.
Ruanne then saw the figure stumbling
Toward them out of light, his head hung down.
Her heart inside her throat, she saw that Cragdon,
A man near death, was struggling alone.
Ruarther was not anywhere in sight,

And then she smelled a bear's rank smell and felt
It rising up inside the forest, light
Cold-deep in red eyes burning hate and rage.
She saw it rise up from the fire's dark ash
And hunch above Ruarther's sleeping body
Burned raw by dragon flame and coal-black rage,
Its roiling spirit flowing like a stream
Into the rage that made it who it was.
The vision made her stagger, sending blackness,
A thin, sharp, liquid arrow at her brain.

Despair rose like sour bile into her throat.
She gasped for breath. She felt malevolence
Inside the spirit bear, its power reaching
Toward reality that pulsed in human hearts.
Ruarther, caught inside its power, danced
As if he were a puppet on a string,
His living bridging chaos, what was real.
She could not save him from the spirit bear.
By finding him she'd only risk herself.

She heard A-Brimm shout when he saw the man.

She watched as Cragdon stopped his movement, tried
To understand if he were hearing things,
And lifted up his head into the air.

She turned toward the village, away from Cragdon
As all the hunters ran toward the man.
She could not see. The great bear smiled at her
And laughed its weirding as she fled its madness,
Ruarther's madness, wondering how she
Could keep him safe from who he was inside,
The terrifying bear inside his skin,
A man who thought that he could kill a child
And bring a peace he'd purposely destroyed.

I should have known, she thought. Ruarther's strength
Was great enough to live through dragon's fire.
Salvation laid in her and not in him.

~ 24 ~

Creating a Dragon Out of Air

Wei waved her arms and saw the dragon grow
Into the winter air, the bones and flesh
Beneath the scales pulsating life so strong
It seemed to meld the blood she felt with blood
Alive and moving through the morning's sun.
Inside her mind she started singing, trying
To bring to life the light that flowed from hands
That conjured particles of shining light
Into a dragon's life, and then her voice,
Reverberating with vast power,
Rang out into the mountains, fields of snow
That burned with light reflected from the sun.

She felt the dragon twist in front of her,
Saw dragon eyes look down into her eyes,
And felt the power in the spells she cast.
She'd never dreamed that she could see a dragon,
Feel deep into its spirit and its bones,
And conjure life from sunlight, empty air.
She felt as large as jagged mountain peaks
That rose majestically above the world.
Her voice rose deep into a dragon's roar.
She breathed her life into the dragon's life.
She reached for chaos where her mother's hands
Were weaving magic through her hands,
But then she felt the dragon's tail begin

To flicker as the whole she tried to hold
Inside her mind began to dissipate.
She quickly moved her hands, solidified
The tail, but as the image firmed, the life
Inside her voice began to skitter, fragment
Into the dance of light above the snow.
She reached out to her mother, tried to find
Her essence in the chaos of the light.

An overwhelming sense of emptiness
Engulfed her, causing her to feel how young
She was, how vulnerable, how lost.
The dragon, formed of light, collapsed as flesh
Became the molecules of nothingness.
The winter day was bright with morning sun.

She tried to find her mother in the maelstrom
Where death whirled clouds of souls into a dance
That had no individual substance, life.
She felt like wailing like a little girl
Whose mother slept deep in her earthen grave.
She held back sobs, got on her feet, and stumbled
Into the cottage to her mother's bed.

Ssruuanne, she told herself. Ssruuanne still lives.
The words inside her head were meaningless.

She tried to see her mother by the bed,
Her form half in the room, a wavering
Between the universe of death and life.
She waved her arms and tried to cast a spell
That penetrated boundaries and let
Her see her mother and her father's light,
But nothing happened. All her power wisped

Into the air and only let her touch
Her mother's bed, an aching emptiness.

She felt the dragon's scale upon her arm
Pulse hot with beating from a dragon's heart.
She stared at where it glowed with dragon life,
A life inside of her that was not her.
Ssruuanne, she thought. Ssruuanne still lives.

The revelation seeped into her like
The rising of the pool where dragonflies
Assembled in the early days of summer.
The dragon scale was part of her, her flesh.
She'd conjured it without Ssruuanne in front
Of her to make her feel how it should be.

She reached out to her mother once again.
She felt the knot of humans waving arms
Inside a wind that was no wind or substance.
She felt despair inside the knot, the sense
The gate they'd made had transferred dragon flesh
Into the world and now was closed for good,
Their power faltering inside the chaos.
Wei sent her mind into the place her mother
Had made outside her deathbed's bleak despair.
The essence of her mother sensed her presence,
Surrounded her with deathless weaves of love.

Stunned, Wei sat on the floor and stared at where
The dragon scale, embedded in her arm,
Throbbed from the beating of a dragon's hearts.
She was alone, she thought: No human friends,
No dragon friends, no family, alone.
The winter cold burned harshness through the world.
She wondered if she'd be alive come spring.

~ 25 ~

Rising Sentience

Inside her cave, emotions traumatised
  From feeling how Wei's eyes had looked at her
  And seemed to strip her essence from her spirit,
Ssruuanne instinctively sent out her thoughts
To Mmirrimann inside his nearby cave.
The ancient dragon dragged his shrouded spirit
Toward his bed beside the cave's deep pool
Exhausted, beaten by his reckless journey.

The sense of Wei's bright eyes beneath her scales
Exploring deep into her dragon's self
Dissolved when Ssruuanne felt the song of chaos
In Mmirrimann's unconsciousness as if
He'd faced his doom and somehow was alive.
The aches she'd felt from feeling violation
Wisped out of her and, with an eagerness
Pushed by a rush of fear, she stood outside,
The mountain winds soft on her golden scales.
What had her ancient lover tried to do?
She leaped to air and glided to his cave.

The leader of the mountain dragons slumped
Onto his bed and stared at golden eyes
That whirled at where his head was pressed to stone.
He tried to order thoughts into his mind,
But images replete with nothingness

And roaring sounds of endless chaos made
Him close his eyes against the fierceness burning
Inside Ssruuanne's vexed, swirling eyes.

He had to live, to leave the nothingness
Infecting what he once had been behind,
But in the chaos, thought was tenuous,
A string of self that could not know itself.
He willed the window from the chaos closed,
But in the cave the stone walls wavered, motes
Solidifying, then dissolving into motes,
Light flickering into his mind, then sweeping
Into the roar of silence swirling, swirling . . .

Ssruuanne stared angrily at Mmirrimann.
He'd gone too far. She saw the journey braved
Past dragon memories into the realms
Where time and living spirits danced in chaos –
More spectres than a memory
Of life once lived upon the living earth.
What will had brought him back into his cave
Was past an understanding she possessed.
His scales seemed insubstantial, light, not flesh.
He did not seem to have the strength to open
His eyes to see the safety that he'd found.

She knew the motivation driving him.
She heard, inside her mind, the rage Sshruunak
Spewed from his mind into his followers,
The great young males that saw his massive strength
And did not see how puny human strength
Had sent him, wounded, fleeing to his cave.
She saw what rage and mindless joy in strength
Had done to dragon lives through time, the long,

Dark spiralling toward a day when dragons
Would be a myth long lost from memory.

His courage blazing, Mmirrimann had braved
The chaos where the spirit beasts brewed life
From nothingness and came to feed
Upon earth-light and human/dragon lives.
He'd tried to find elixirs that would lead
The mountain dragons past the young males' rage
Into a future guarding dragon eggs
And dragon wings and dragon sentience.

He'd thought that in the memories he carried
Of generations born from dragon eggs
An answer waited with deliverance,
But he had gone too far, his love of dragons
Enticing him into the realms of death.

"You are a fool," Ssruuanne said. "Just a fool."

She walked into his cave and pressed her scales
Against his scales and tried to warm the cold
Chilled deep into his spirit by the wind
That was no wind, the place of deathless souls.
She forced her warmth into his cold and strained
To find the order still inside his mind
And tried to reach the will that he had used
To bring his body back into his cave.

"The dragon race is not gone yet," she said,
Her voice an echo in the small, close cave.
She felt his reaching out toward her warmth.
She forced her thoughts of Wei to disappear
And placed a block upon Sshruunak's dark thoughts

To keep them out of Mmirrimann, his cold.
She lay beside him on his stone-smooth bed
And sent him memories of watching eggs
As hatchlings struggled out of large blue shells
From darkness into light and dragon life.
She felt again the joy at seeing life begin,
The promise of another generation.
She nestled close and soaked his cold with warmth
As hours passed day toward the winter night.

"You'll live," she told him in the ancient tongue.
"We'll face Sshruunak and keep the war
He's brewed from ever happening. We will."

He formed a thought, then lost its substance, fought
Toward his sentience, fell back, then felt
Ssruuanne beside him in his mountain cave.
He saw a golden dragon hovering
Outside the light the human shamans made
To make the bridge between the void and life.
He reached toward her warmth and living mind.
He loved her. She loved him. A thought
And feeling formed inside the chaos, let
Him feel her body pressed against his body.
He sighed his rising sentience and grinned.

~ 26 ~

Plotting Human Extinction

The darkness, black as scales upon Sshruunak,
   Awash with atmospheres that breathed unrest,
   Intensified inside the mountain valley,
Hid one great dragon, then another, then
Another spreading silent wings to land
Into a ring of black obsidian boulders.
Sshruunak, placed in the ring's dead centre, glared
At every dragon as they flared their wings
And settled in a loop around his force.

No dragon spoke, but waited for Sshruunak.
The wounded male puffed fire to smoke the air.
It let them see each other in the dark,
But only briefly as Sshruunak began
To speak inside his mind about his plans.

"The humans cannot live," he said. "Their minds
Are dangerous to dragonkind, their tools
As evil as their deadliness and hate.
I've learned," he said, his voice still silent, "how
Our strength is not enough to make them cower.
They swarm like wasps inside a paper hive
And pour out on the ground with deadly arrows
As if their puny bodies calculate
The end of dragons' lives lived on the earth.
I've lost an eye and feel the pain they bring

To every dragon who has sense to rage
Against abomination in our midst.

"I've brooded long," he said. "I've seen their power.
I've seen that if we try to use our strength,
Our fiery breath, our flight, our deadly claws,
To end the peril that they represent,
We'll end up fertilizing earth in graves.
Old Mmirrimann is not the fool he seems.
Ssruuanne's geas capturing our spirits
Burns from a knowledge born of memories
And senses I have never known or dreamed."

His rumbling stopped. The long necks of the others
Stopped moving from the trance he'd woven tight
About them, capturing them through his mind.
At last, the silence lengthening, Ssshraann,
The dragon closest to Sshruunak, his red,
Dark scales dull in the valley's darkness, sneered.
"And so we hide inside our caves and let the humans
Grow stronger year by year as dragons weaken?"
He shook his massive head and almost grinned.
"That's not Sshruunak," he said, his voice intense.

Sshruunak stayed silent, but his voice rang out
Inside his head and stunned the other males.

"The humans swarm like ants or wasps," he said.
"And then they use their tools to penetrate
Our scales and seek our vulnerabilities."
He paused, his eye alight with swirling colours.
"Each dragon feels their power in their hearts.
We breathe our fire and spread our massive wings
And throw ourselves at puny, boiling ants

And rend and tear their flesh and spill their blood
In gallons on the ground and murder them.
But never do the dragons swarm and boil
Like wasps stirred from a threatened nest,
And so we fly into their stinging arrows
And die as solitary as our spirits.
We murder them, but let their numbers murder
Each one of us as if we were alone."

Ssshraann, russet dark, the strongest of the males,
Moved nervously inside the circle, eyes
Intense, his thoughts a worry on his face.
"We learn to form an army like the humans?"
He asked. "Act like a clutch of insubstantial fools?"

Sshruunak raged fire into the night, his breath
So hot it penetrated dragon hides.
The great snow covered peaks around the valley
Grew even darker as his fire went on and on.
He roared so loud an avalanche began
To crash in distance down a mountainside.
The males, eyes glittering, stared amazed
At dragon power unleashed into the world.

The silence following the roar was sudden,
A chaos filled with dreadful absences.
Sshruunak's great head bowed down toward the snow
Inside the circle of obsidian.
He spoke out loud, his voice as soft as snow
Descending slowly out of windless skies.

"I see us flying in a full moon's golden light,"
He said. "As silent as my voice is now."
He glared at Ssshraann, inviting opposition.

The russet dragon seemed to be onboard,
His angry doubt quailed by Sshruunak's dark force.

"We're primed with fire and human discipline.
Each one has targets to attack and kill.
Each one of us is bound by orders planned
So that we decimate our enemies.
We come upon a human town and swoop
Into the human helplessness and burn
Their leaders as they try to form defence
Against a threat they've never thought would come.
I see our legions wing into their mass,
Our darkness deadly, purpose aimed and armed
With knowledge born of dragon strength and wiles.
I see the humans dying like the ants they are,
Their villages and towns black, smoking ruins."

Ssshraann grinned inside the darkness, showed his teeth,
And looked into Sshruunak's bright, whirling eye,
The charring where his other eye had been.
He felt the dragon army forming in the night.
Around him, Drressel, Stoormachen, Waanderlund,
The leading males born since the human peace,
Born in the caves, half danced with the vision
Of dragons massed into an army, flying
Through moonlit skies toward the final answer
To humans and their domination of the earth.

~ 27 ~

Escaping Possession

Ruarther woke to sunlit cold, his head
So sore he felt as if his life were bound
Inside the thrumming pain that made him scowl.
The burns were gone from arms, legs, chest,
And though he felt as if he could not move,
His spirit rose to know that he'd survived.
The fire beside the boulder smouldered, smoke
Still rising from the cold, grey, lumpy ash.
He stirred up from the hollow in the snow
He'd made for sleep and, groaning, found his pack
And put a slice of jerky in his mouth.
The goat was strong beneath the heavy spice,
But he had never tasted food so good.
He was alive and eating, wolfing meat
That tasted sweet as honey on his tongue.

He looked toward the campfire, felt the cold,
And thought he'd build it up and warm his hands,
But then he picked his pack up, shouldered it,
And started climbing through the dazzling fields.
He'd not find where the witch's cottage was
Before the sun blazed down, he told himself.
He'd better move before his will had failed,
And warmth became the cause for lethargy.
He'd never kill the child by staying put.
The surface of the snow had frozen hard.

He moved as swiftly as his legs could move.
He did not sink each time he took a step.
The walking cleared his head and made him feel
As if he'd found his humanness again.
He thanked the spirit bear inside his mind,
Exhilarated at the strength he felt.

But then, just miles from where the cliffs rose black
Into the winter's white, he stopped, confused.
The air in front of him looked charged, a mass
Of swirling chaos threatening to end
The world's solidity with nothingness.
He felt the bear rear up inside the chaos,
Felt snow and fields and light sucked to the dark.

A woman, waving hands, had somehow grabbed
The bear with energies Ruarther felt,
But could not see, a battle raging far
Beyond his senses even though he sensed
The powers devastating what was real,
Miasma threatening existence anchored
To life he'd always thought was all that was.
He stepped back as the chaos inched toward
Where he had stopped, the swirling wild with songs
Originating from beyond existence.

A greater fear than what he'd felt the day
He'd faced the golden dragon seized his heart.
He saw the bear's face waver in the light
And then the woman's weaving web of hands
As death came from its natural place and tried
To build a portal to Ruarther's world.
He wondered why he'd left his days-old camp
To face a wilderness he'd thought was myth.

The great bear turned away from chaos, stared
At where Ruarther stood in front of him
Inside the realness of the real world
And leaped toward the body with a heart.

The witch is doing this, Ruarther thought.
The witch! He tried to dive away from where
The bear had aimed his leap, but even though
He moved as fast as any human could,
Convulsions ripped his consciousness.
He owed the bear, he thought. He owed the bear.

He fought against the spirit entering
His spirit, tried to be the self he was,
But in his mind the great bear roared and roared.
Time wavered as the sunlight flared, then died,
Then flared alive again, the chaos mixed
With life's stability, existence swelling
With spectres lost beyond the boundaries
Of what could ever be or come to be.

The child, Ruarther raged inside himself,
The witch's child had made the dragon mock
Him as he hunted in the woods that day,
And now she'd witched the bear into his spirit.
He'd kill the child, he roared. He'd kill the girl.

The spirit in him roared against his roar.
Ruarther felt the self he knew recoil
As chaos swirled into his head and bones.
I'm stronger than the bear, he snarled inside.
The bear seemed bigger than the universe.
His heart beat crazily, his fear
The only rage that kept him from possession,

The end of who he was, a human man.
I'll kill the girl, he chanted in his head.
The witch's girl is dead. I'll kill the girl.

The great bear twisted as it fought to find
A place away from where the woman's hands
Wove order out of chaos with chaotic song.
Ruarther twisted painfully in snow
So cold it seemed to burn his throbbing flesh.
He felt as if he were inside a furnace,
The brick kiln burning with a glowing heat,
His skin so sensitive it seared with pain,
As if he'd touched a fiery red-hot coal
And spread its agony across his face,
Hours blistering into eternity.

The bear retreated from the searing pain,
Life's sharpness shredding who it was
Into the emptiness of air and sky.
Chaotic swirling dissipated into mist.
The sunlit cold possessed the world again.
Ruarther, body still, stunned, felt his life
Inside the who of who he was, a man.

Splayed out upon the snow, his body laying
Where he had fallen even though he'd been
Oblivious to falling down, he wondered
How he had thought he had the strength to kill
A witch so powerful she had the force
To bend a dragon's spirit to her will,
A witch who made a spirit bear afraid
And conjured it into the life of earth.
He felt so tired he could not lift himself
Off snow to stand and move from where he was.

He could not countenance that he still lived
Outside of deathless chaos in his world.

~ 28 ~

Conversation: From Love Through Fear

As Mmirrimann stirred, lost in ancient times,
A great green dragon in a cave as dusky
As scales that gleamed inside the daylight's dark,
He felt Ssruuanne beside him, sending life
Into the dreams that tried to capture him
And let him drift away into forgetfulness.
Then, slicing through his dream as if a claw
Had separated clouds, revealing sky,
An image of a valley high above
The caves, beneath a shining silver moon,
Filled up the emptiness inside of him.

He opened up his eyes and saw Ssruuanne,
Her head raised up, her eyes awhirl with colours,
Engaged with all the images that flooded
Through Mmirrimann and welcomed him to life.

He stirred, his thoughts replete with shadowed shapes
And concentrated on his long-time love.
She saw his grin and puffed a ring of smoke
Into the darkness of the icy cave.

"What did you find?" she asked inside her head.

He looked away from eyes that seemed to scald
His life with endless memories, the two of them,

Wings filled with power, spiralling toward
The summer sun as passion trumpeted
Their fervour to the mountain peaks below.

"The mother of the girl has built a bridge
Of power in the purgatorial space
Where winds that are no winds blow in a gale,"
He grumbled deep inside his massive chest.
"She needs to save her child and interrupts
The natural order of the universe."

Ssruuanne stayed still and let her body's heat
Send life into the love she'd cherished through
The human wars into the days of peace.

"The geas is right?" she asked. "The child must live?"

"I took the woman's bridge from nothingness,"
He answered. "When I passed I'm sure the bridge
Disintegrated into nothingness."

"It's over then? The child has lost her powers?"

"Sshruunak has left his cave and gathers males
Around him for another human war,"
He said, the image of the valley bathed
In silver light inside his head. "I felt
The rage the witch felt when I used her bridge.
She'll not give up. She'll make another bridge."

Ssruuanne looked at the smudge of morning light
That tinged a small cloud's underside outside
The cave, dawn grey and cold with winter winds.
"How can you build a bridge between the veil

That separates reality from death?"
She asked. "I know the spirit beasts can find
A moment anchored in our time, but they
Are insubstantial, not quite corporeal."

"Perhaps the child should perish," Mmirrimann
Said softly. "But I fear the forces spinning
From where I was into this world or ours.
I don't believe the dragon race can live
Unless we find a way to live in peace.
The human girl is like a keystone strong
Inside a wall, but if it's taken out,
The wall will crumble to a pile of dust.
Sshruunak can send all that we've built to dust."

Ssruuanne looked long at him and hummed her fear.

"We're old," she said. "Sshruunak can char our scales."

"He's gathering a dragon army, figuring
He'll use the tactics made by human wiles
To waste the villages and towns that sprout
Like mushrooms all across the wilderness."

"The deathless realms will fill with spirits then,"
She said. "Both dragons and their human foes
Will die in droves. As dragons we won't win."

"Sshruunak has left the caves and won't be back
Until he's built his dragon army, ravening
Across the landscape like a fiery scythe."

Ssruuanne's scales rippled her distress that made
Her move from Mmirrimann. He did not move.

"We'll face our doom," he said at last. "I need
To rest and think about experiencing
The winds of purgatory, what I've learned.
I did not journey past my memories
To die," he said. "I trekked to find a path
That leads to dragons hatching out of eggs
Into the glories of a dragon's life."

~ 29 ~

Unexpected Warning

For four whole days Ruanne stayed in her cottage,
Her mind obsessed with understanding how
Ruarther had decided that he'd keep
His vile intent to kill Crayllon's young child.
When Reestor knocked and called to her, she sat
Inside her rocking chair, her energy
So sapped she could not force herself to move.
When Old Broar came she listened to his voice
And told herself she ought to answer him,
But as she tried to force herself to move,
She lost her will and fled into a place
Where silence made her feel as if she were
A stone, a weight too ponderous to stir.

What's wrong with me? she thought. How can I sit
When in the wilderness Ruarther stalks
A child, and dragons calculate how fire
Will rain upon the village that I love?
Why can't I find some energy to act?
To try to talk to dragons, let them know
The humans want to keep the peace alive?

She got up from the chair, her restlessness
So powerful it seemed to make her move.
I need to sleep, she thought. Or maybe die.
The thought of suicide hit like a bolt

Of lightning, coursing through her sluggish blood.
She'd been so positive, determined that she'd find
Ruarther, keep him safe, end threats from dragons,
And shield Crayllon's child from Ruarther's rage.
She sat down on the bed and longed to end
Insomnia and all the doubts that crowded
Into her head and took away her rationality.
She been awake for days, she thought. For days.

She laid down, closed her eyes, the universe
A journey in the dark toward a place
Where aeons spiralled ever outward, past
Her consciousness into an emptiness.
She felt the witches born before her birth,
A fire in blood that ran through centuries,
Their hands and spells alive with ancient power.

A darkness overwhelmed her, made her feel
Alone, as worthless as a woman lost.
But then she felt a rhythm in the dark.
Hands wove a web into the nothingness.
A woman's hands had grabbed a spirit bear,
Translating from one world into the next,
Her passion fashioning a passageway
Between the purgatory of the dark
And sunlight stretched across great fields of snow.
She felt Ruarther's rage strike at the bear . . .

And then she felt a dragon's curious mind
Invade her like a boiling swarm of bees,
His hugeness startled at the spark she sent
Across the fields into a darkened cave.
Her body shook to feel intelligence
That poked at her as if her insignificance

Were novel, hardly to be countenanced.

This was not like before, she thought. She felt
The other dragon's startlement to feel her presence
So unexpectedly inside his mind.
The vision that she'd sent had been a gift.

Inside this dragon's thought she forced herself
Away from where she'd been inside her bed
And, sloughing off her lethargy, discovered
The fire of who she was, a woman wild
Enough to set off in the wilderness
To find the only man she'd ever loved.
It seemed as if the dragon's massive mind
Had sparked alive her energy and self.

She felt the dragon staring at her mind.
He did not speak, but stirred out of his thoughts
To see what human was confronting him.
He sounded tired, as if he'd lost his energy,
His will to face another dawning day.
At last he said, "And who are you?" his voice
So loud inside her head it made her tremble.

She looked into his eyes out at his cave
And wondered how she saw across the miles.
She could not think. His hugeness was too large.
The other dragon had been half his size.
He waited, looking patiently at her.
She felt a panic rising up into her throat.
"Who are you?" she demanded, wondering
At how she'd found the bravery to speak.

The dragon blinked. "I'm Mmirrimann," he said.

"I ask again: And who are you that's brave
Enough to face a dragon in his lair?"

His words unnerved Ruanne. Mmirrimann?
The leader dragon that had made the peace?
The murderer of Reestor's father? Legend
That spoke to her as if she were alive?

"The humans do not want a war," she said,
The mission given her by Reestor flooding
Into her head. "Our children need to live."

The dragon blinked again. Inside his eyes,
So alien to human eyes, Ruanne believed
She sensed a sadness powerful beyond
The human sadness that was troubling her.

"I too would like to keep the peace," he said.
"But I am old, and younger males see war
As part of what a dragon ought to be.
You'd better let your leaders know my words.
I cannot stop the war to come though I
Would give my years to see continuous peace.
War's near, and though I'll try to keep its rage
From ending dragon life, I've searched, but found
No way to stop the conflagration's fires."

He looked away. The emptiness returned.
Ruanne stared at her hands clutched in her lap.
The greatest dragon that had ever lived
Could find no way to stop the war Ruarther,
In madness, had engendered from his rage?

Someone was pounding at her cottage door.

"Ruanne? Ruanne?" a worried Reestor called.
"You can't hide from the world, Ruanne," he said.

Ruanne remembered sadness in the eyes
That stared so powerfully into her eyes.
She got up, went to open up the door.

~ 30 ~

Another Dragon Scale

Beside the pond's white, frozen face, the sound
   Of water from the stream beneath the ice
   A muffled music in the morning air,
Wei waved her arms and conjured motes
Of fire congealing to a dragon's shape.
She strained to make the dragon breathe with scales
As golden as Ssruuanne's great shimmering.
She concentrated, gathering the whole
Of who she was into the spell she wove.
The motes of light began to coalesce.
The dragon in the air took shape, its eyes
So bright they nearly seemed to be alive.
Wei felt the power in her young girl's body
Sweep out of her into the dragon's head,
Its nostrils flaring as she tried to find
A dragon's breath in dragon lungs beneath
The light she wove into the winter air . . .

But then, just like the other times, the motes
Of light collapsed into a day's blue skies.
She held the eyes a moment as they looked
At her, their golden green intelligence,
But even though she danced her hands and wove
Her body as she tried to find the power
That let the spell she'd made exist in time,
The dragon eyes scattered into nothingness.

The irritation that she felt was strong
Enough to make her want to cry, but deep
Inside she knew that if the tears began,
They'd wrack her body, bringing weariness
That would not let her try to form a dragon
From air again for days and maybe weeks.

She shook her head and felt the warmth the sun
Was pouring down onto the fields of snow.
A hint of spring was in the air although
Real spring was still at least a month away.
Why did she feel as if she had to craft
A dragon from the still-fresh memories
Ssruuanne had left inside of who she was?
What kind of girl had she become? Her mother's
Ethereal spirit once alive, now gone?
Her body thin enough so that it seemed
As if a puff of wind could scatter her
Just like the dragons that she'd tried to make
Evaporated into empty air?

She sighed and turned away from where the sun
Would shine upon the pond's still face in spring
And walked to where the woodpile stood and took
Two chunks of wood into the cottage-warmth.
She put one piece upon the fire and watched
As flames licked up its sides through rising smoke.
Why had her mother's ghost not come again?
She asked herself. Where had her mother gone?

She shook her head and picked the rabbit laying
Beside the sink up by its large hind legs.
The trap she'd made from fire had kept her fed
As winter kept its grip upon the land.

Strong spelling had its uses. That was sure.

She took a knife out of the drawer, started
The job of skinning rabbit fur and hide,
And thought about her coming birthday, how
It would not mean what once it would have meant.
She'd get no presents, eat no special meal.
She missed her mother, not the spectral form
That taught her spells out of her earthen grave –
Her living mother quick to comfort her.

She put the knife down, poured some water, washed
Her hands and quietly walked to her bed.
She'd never heard of anyone with power
Enough to make a dragon out of air,
But still, she felt as if she ought to breathe
And work her spells and feel a dragon's life
Flow from her hands into a living dragon.

She sat down on the bed and looked at where
The dragon's scale was burned into her arm.
A bunch of normal kids would stare at her,
Then scream and run away to see the scale,
She thought. They'd know that she was strange.

She waved her arm above her head and felt
The scale grow warm. She moved both arms and felt
A spell grow in the air, its power stirring
Inside the cottage, stimulating life.
She started humming underneath her breath
And broke into a song that trilled and soared
And made her feel her power once again.
She was a girl, she thought. A girl. A girl.

A square beside the scale she wore began
To burn her flesh; she felt the fire inside
Her arm and felt a second scale begin
To grow beside the first, a dragon's life
Inside her life, out of her life, a dragon . . .

She stopped and let her arms fall from the air
And let the silence come back to the room.
She held her arm up, stared at where two scales
Lay side by side, their gold burned in her arm.
She waved her arm and tried to feel if it
Was heavier than it had been before.
It felt as if it were her arm, but looked
As strange as any arm had ever looked.

What kind of girl had she become? she asked.
She felt the movements of the fate
That waited her and felt as strong and fierce
As any dragon born out of an egg.

~ 31 ~

The Valley of the Scorched Black Stones

The great black dragon banked and hurtled down
　　Toward the ring of valley stones, his silence
　　So disciplined and fierce it seemed a fire
Inside his belly ready to be flamed.
Behind his plummeting Ssshraann and eight
Great dragons followed, silent, disciplined,
Intent on coming on their enemies
So unexpectedly they'd have no time
To organise an orderly defence.

A hundred feet above the stone, Sshruunak
Swerved hard, his flame scorched black into the circle
Inside the cold, black stones, and soared back up
Into the air, each dragon following
Emitting flame at different spots pre-planned
Before the drill had started in the dark.
Around the stones the earth was bare and soft
In spite of ten-foot snows inside the valley.

Sshruunak veered from the circle to a pattern
Where claws extended to the ground and flame
Burst down into the hordes of pretend men,
Death chortling inside his hearts as chaos
Defeated enemies as old as dragonkind.
Behind him every dragon took a pattern
That spiralled from the centre out to points

Designed to make their enemies despair.
Sshruunak then trumpeted retreat and flew
Toward the rendezvous inside a hollow
Below a great, snow-covered mountain peak.

Inside the hollow in a wind that howled,
He grinned to see each dragon land exactly
As he had ordered them to land, their eyes
Awhirl with colours fiery with delight.
The dragons planned. Their days of passiveness
Inside the mountain caves were nearly done.
The joy of rage and battle lust was burning
In dragon hearts and dragon strength again.

The eight great males around him waited, eyes
Locked on his eyes, their frenzy disciplined
By how he'd forged their senses to his will.

"We're ready," he announced, his triumph edged
Into his voice. "We'll wait until the moon
Is new and blacker than my scales, then strike
The village near to where we've cowered all
The years since Mmirrimann invoked his peace.
We'll see how strong our tactics are before
We use our skills and strength to decimate
The King of Tryon's vaunted capital."

He paused. "We'll win this war and start to end
The humans' dominance," he said. "But when
We burn the village to the ground, we need
To see that every human in the village dies.
We need to test what we have learned, but if
A single human gets away, they'll flee
And warn the armies that the peace is done.

We won't possess surprise, a weapon needed
With only nine to score a victory.

"Ssruuanne and Mmirrimann still lead the dragons.
To win the war we need the ones that hide
And live their lives in peace inside the caves.
To bring them to the war we have to kill
Each woman, child, and man inside the village
Or else face armies greater than our numbers
Can beat inside Tyron's stone city gates."

Stoormachen smiled and shook his head. "I am
A dragon male," he said. "I won't hold back
From tasting human blood and crunching bones."

"We'll hide until the night of blackness comes,"
Ssshraann said. "Then we will meet inside the circle,
As you have said, and start another war."

"We'll end the human dominance and breed
Like dragons ought to breed in open air,"
Sshruunak said. "We will make an age that dragons
Will celebrate as long as dragons live!"

Stoormachen roared as nine great dragons let
Their voices smash into the mountainsides
And loose great tides of snow in avalanches
That roared back at their thunderous roars.

"To victory!" Sshruunak screeched. Then he flapped
His wings and shot into the air and flew
Toward the valley of the scorched black stones.

~ 32 ~

Doubt

Ruarther struggled to his feet confused, his head
A swirling mass of vertigo that made
Him feel as if he'd left the world and found
A state of being where the dead and living
Danced crazily between reality
And purgatory's grey, miasmic void.
The sun was going down, and as he thought
About the spirit bear and how its strength
Had battered him, attempting to possess
The self he knew was who he'd always been,
He also knew the night would rage with cold
And threaten him with all the swirling mass
That seemed to make it difficult to stand.
He had to find a sheltered place to build
A fire or else not see another dawn.

At last he stood, a tottering old man
Whose will to live was interlinked with rage.
The thought that he had never seen the child
Who plagued him like a meme caught in his head
Disquieted him, made the swirling chaos
Inside his mind unbalance how he stood.
He felt his body weave as if a wave
Had flowed beneath the snow unsteadying
His capability to stand upright.
He had to move, he thought. Before he fell.

He took a step toward the mountains, paused,
Then forced another step, the day's last light
So blinding that he turned his head away.
Out of the corner of his eye he glimpsed
A copse of pines dark in the sunset's fire.
He changed direction, stumbled awkwardly
Across the hard-crust snow toward the pines.

And then he stopped. He felt the spirit bear
Inside the murkiness in front of him.
The bear was in the void, a monstrous shape
That had no form, but whirled into a wind
That was no wind, a shape that struggled through
A turbulence that formed a boundary
Against its will and need to be alive.

Ruarther braced himself to feel the strength
The bear could batter at his grasp of self.
The bear had healed his body. Now it stalked
Him as he tried to find a place to start a fire.
The turbulence grew larger as it swirled,
But then it disappeared as if its winds
Had flashed into the void, home to the bear.
There was no sense the witch's ghost was near.

Ruarther forced his legs to move again.
He concentrated on the copse of pines
Inside the sunset's fiery light and lost
The sense of fear he'd felt for endless days.
He felt as if a weight had been removed.
He touched the bow inside its leather case.
He stopped again. Above the mountain peaks
A black dot flew toward him through the air.
He felt malevolence that emanated

From where the dragon flashed in sunset's fire.
He did not want to be upon the plains
Defenceless as the dragon hunted prey.
He forced himself to run toward the copse
In spite of how his running made the world
Swim round and round before unfocused eyes.

The time was near, he told himself. He felt
The dragons practising their ancient skills,
Anticipating how they, at long last,
Could end continuance of human life.
He had to kill the witch's child, he thought.
He had to end the threat all humans faced.

At last the pines grew larger as he ran.
He gasped for breath and tried to keep the world
From reaching up and slamming him to ground.
The pine trees welcomed him into their dusk.
He found a sheltered spot beside a trunk
Long fallen to the ground and built a fire.
As fingers trembled just above the flame,
He wondered why he thought the child had sent
The golden dragon searching for him when
He'd run away and hidden in the woods.
The witch was dead. That's what the dragon said.
The child was young and needed human care.

Perhaps the child was dead, he thought. Perhaps . . .
But then he felt the child across the miles
Inside her cottage by a warming fire.
He tried to puzzle out the feeling that he had,
But all he knew was that the child still lived.
There was a link between the golden dragon
And witch's child, he thought. The coal-black dragon

Was deep in plans for devastating war.

He stared at how the fire he'd built woke up
The dark and made it dance with leaping shadows.
Doubts gnawed at him inside the shadow dance.
He looked up at the sky. The waning moon
Cast little light, intensified the cold.
He took his blankets from his deer hide pack
And put more wood upon the growing fire.

He'd make the peace, he told himself. I'll kill
The witch's child and end the dragon threat.
He wondered why the spirit bear was blocked
From coming to the earth and walking where
Its kind had always walked through haunted light.

~ 33 ~

Mmirrimann Inside the Conclave He Called

One

The weirding shocked Ssruuanne awake and stirred
Inside of her a fear that made her hearts
A double drum vibrating in her bones.
Beside her Mmirrimann was sleeping like
A dragon slept, not like a dragon caught
Inside miasma's cold, chaotic winds.
He twitched to feel her movement, stirred,
But stayed asleep, his eyelids fluttering.
She softly moved away from him and stood
Upon the ledge outside his cave, her eyes
As restless as the beating of her hearts.
She spread her wings and launched into the air.

Disturbances seemed everywhere, the signs
Of abnormality small waves in draughts
Beneath the surface of her golden wings.
She looked toward Wei's cottage, felt the weirding
That seemed frustrated as the human girl
Attempted magic far beyond her skill;
Then turned her neck toward a copse of pine
That seemed to swirl with chaos not unlike
The chaos Mmirrimann had fled to find
His life again inside the dragon caves.
The swirling seemed to buffet her with winds

That were no winds, rappelling her to heights
She hardly ever tried to reach in flight.
Behind her, deep inside the mountains, stones
Scorched black from dragon fire grew tangible
Inside her mind, their silence testament
To how the dragon race would face extinction.
She shuddered at the death they emanated
Into the cold, high beauty of their valley.

Downhill she felt the fear inside the humans
That huddled in their village cottages,
But also felt the strength infused in bows
They'd use to face unwanted dragon threat.

They would not face Sshruunak oblivious
And unprepared, she thought. His plans had gone
Awry without his knowing once again.

The clarion call from Mmirrimann inside
The caves stirred deep in dragon blood and tipped
Her wings so powerfully she almost plunged
Toward the fields of snow beneath her flight.
Her neck whipped round toward the ancient call
And wheeled her in the air toward the caves.

She shuddered at the implications buried
Inside the call, the threat of dragon war
Where dragons faced each other in the skies
And tried to force their will through claws and fire
Into the hearts of spirit, sentience.

How had their peace devolved to this? She thought.

Two

They all were there: The eight huge elders sat
Upon the round, black dais, their eyes a-swirl
With patterns troubling to look at, each
One grim with seeing Mmirrimann perched high
Above them on the perch where, during peace,
Ssruuanne, the oldest one alive, presided.
Before the eight of them the dragon race
Was gathered, restless, angry, filled with fear
Born from a dread that overwhelmed the hall.

Ssruuanne walked in the massive cavern
And took her place below her lover's mass.
He'd shed the weariness he'd felt before
And looked as if he'd never faced a time
He doubted his own strength and dominance.

"The younger males are stirring dragon blood,"
He said, "and taking on another war
That adds another chapter in the long,
Long history of battling the human race.

"I've journeyed deep into our memories
And tried to see if they could find a way
To victory that would not threaten death
To dragonkind," he said. "But in the chaos
Where death is gathered in an endless storm,
I saw despair without a shred of hope
If human/dragon war erupts again.
I've called the call against our senseless sons
Not out of love for humans, but for eggs
Still incubating in the birth cave's warmth.

"If any can convince Sshruunak that he
Must not continue in his path, I ask
You for your words and passion. Otherwise
I've seen no way that dragons will survive.
The puny humans are like swarms of wasps
That sting and sting no matter how we sear
Their lives with dragon strength and claws and fire.
I've warred upon them time and time again,
But dragons dwindle every time we choose
To face our foe with war instead of peace.

"We must choose peace to build our population's strength.
That's what I found inside miasma's chaos.
I saw no other way to keep our eggs alive."

The nine great elders stared into the mass
Of dragon eyes that whirled perplexity.
Those gathering inside the cavern seemed
So numerous it looked as if predictions
Of near extinction had to be a jest.
As Mmirrimann kept staring at the eyes
That stared at him, a clutch of males positioned
Toward the passages into the cavern,
As silently as possible, began
To turn and leave the hall to join Sshruunak.
Wwilliama sighed so loud she forced Ssruuanne
To turn her head to look at her dismay.
At least another dozen males had left.

At last, his voice so sad it seemed to flood
Miasma from the chaos through the hall,
His whirling eyes uncertain, Mmirrimann
Rose to his hind legs, larger than Sshruunak
Of any other male alive, and roared,

"We cannot fail. We must succeed. To war!
To war against our brothers and our sons
And all their unwise dance with dragon deaths!"

~ 34 ~

Human Preparations for War

One

Inside the village Reestor looked around.
   Upon the rooftops men and women worked
   To layer slate slabs from a quarry found
By hunters not too far away, the grey,
Cold stone a barrier against a dragon's flame.
Ruanne had hit upon the idea, fear
So strong inside of her she seemed a fire
Of schemes designed to keep the village safe
From beasts so strong they could not be defeated.

She'd come from facing Mmirrimann's huge mind
Inspired with mystic schemes to keep the village
Alive as dragon flame and claws wracked down
Upon the villagers with furious death.
She'd rocked within her rocking chair and prayed
To sweet Selen, and, like a dragon, drew
Old knowledge from the well of witchery.
She felt strange winds blow wisps of mist
Into her head, her thoughts more air than substance,
Then, in a trance, began to sing and speak.

She'd told about the slate upon the roofs
And then began to formulate a mix
Of oil and chemicals into a tar
That had inside its mix a liquid fire.

She'd spoke out loud and framed a strategy
For facing dragons raging from the skies.

Hours later, when the trance had burned away
Into an afternoon of normal light,
She'd gone into the village hall and found
The oil and chemicals they'd need to mix,
Then shown a group of men the weirdness when
She'd shot an arrow at the village walls
And grimly smiled to see a splash of flames
That burned ferociously on mortared stone.

"We'll dip our arrows in this muck," she'd said.
"A dragon's scales will burn when arrows strike
And make them feel the pain they'll burn in us."

The dozen men who'd trailed Ruanne to stand
And watch her shoot unnatural arrows, blanched
To see the fire that burned the wall's dark stones –
But then they thought about a dragon's flames.
Emotions wrenched their faces, rejecting magic,
Then feeling rapture at the thought that men
Had weapons strong enough to cause a dragon's death.

Two

As Reestor listened half afraid and awed,
The two emotions spilling through uneasiness,
He started following the lead Ruanne
Was spitting out with storms of urgent words.

He wondered what insanity Ruarther
Concocted as he tried to kill the child
He blamed for all the trouble he had caused.

The idea that the greatest hunter ever
Had lost reality and had become
An inadvertent enemy of those
He'd always served was like a nail in flesh.
The thought burned through the days and pulsed its fire
Into the fabric Reestor felt was life.

The memories of death brought by the claws
And fire of dragons still dwelt deep inside.
For years his heart had thundered every time
He'd seen a dragon fly above his head.
He'd seen the houses in the city burn
And heard the anguished cries of children raked
By dragon claws or burned with dragon flames.
Upon the ground, his eyes fixed on the roofs
Ruanne believed would guard against the fire
A dragon's flame could rage into the village,
He mourned days lost when peace was like a stream
That let his people live in lives not doomed
To endless hours of cowering and fear.

Old Broar appeared beside him, dressed in hides
Designed to keep him warm while travelling.

"Ruanne has asked if I will go and tell
King Clayton that the dragons are about
To break the peace," he said. "I hate to go.
I'm way too old, but every man and woman
Is needed here. At least this makes me useful."

The thought of Broar caught by a winter storm
Unsettled Reestor, made him clutch his friend's
Thin arm; his eyes locked with Broar's ancient eyes.
Broar seemed half cheerful at the thought that he

Could still be useful in emergencies.

"You're needed," Reestor said at last. "A blessing
To men as old as you and I, I guess."

Broar smiled. "The storms will stay away," he said.
"I'm not a young man, but I'm tough the way
Old men are always tough, in spirit-heart."

Above them on the roof a hunter yelped.
He'd cut his hand by sliding slate in place.
When Reestor looked back down at Broar, he'd walked
Away toward the village's stone gates.

Good luck, my friend, he thought. Walk sure and strong.

He glanced toward the mountains bright with sun.
There were no dragons in the skies. He wondered
What storms were brewing in the caverns' dark.

If Mmirrimann was old, he still was strong
Enough to make his will a force no dragon,
Or human, could afford to disregard.
He'd let Ruanne know that he disapproved
Of human/dragon war. He would not let
Events occur without his presence felt.
The old male once had seemed to Reestor like
The heart of evil aimed against mankind,
But now he seemed as if he were a bulwark
Against a war that Reestor prayed would end
Before a human life had been destroyed.

Before a dragon or a human life
Had been destroyed, he prompted silently.

Before a human or a dragon life.

He looked down at A-Brimm's young son, his eyes
Excited at the bustle on the roofs.

"Another load," the young man said. He pointed
Toward where men were pulling steadily
A sled of dark grey slate into the gate.
"We'll show those dragons, won't we Reestor, sir?"

The anguish on his brother's frightened face,
Unwanted, suddenly appeared to Reestor.
The huge, green dragon roared as flame peeled off
His father's face and left his skull hot, red
Upon the roof the two of them were on.

The child stepped back, afraid, and Reestor forced
The terror on his face away and smiled.

"We'll be prepared," he told the boy, his voice
As gentle as a soft, spring wind. "The dragons won't . . ."
He paused.   "We'll greet them with a storm of arrows,"
He said. "A deadly storm of human arrows."

The boy looked at him, hesitant, then smiled.
"We humans aren't afraid," he said. "We're not."

Without responding Reestor looked toward
The distant mountains and forgot to smile.

~ 35 ~

Vertigo and the Moment of Sudden Truth

One

He woke as groggy as he'd ever felt,
   Miasma thick inside the sheltering copse.
   The fire he'd built was smouldering as light
Crept through the branches to the snowy ground.
He forced himself to sit, then slowly stood,
The weirding powerful enough to change
The way the trees looked as he tried to find
His balance in a universe that seemed to roll
Across a land with waves beneath its soils.

I have to kill the witch's child, he said
Into a wilderness that did not hear.

He bent and carefully picked up his bow
And sheaf of arrows, then walked warily
Out of the copse into the fields of snow.
He had to orient himself toward
The cabin where the witch had made her home,
But then felt better as he slowly made his way
Across the blinding fields of crusted white.

A half-mile from the copse he felt a wave
Of nausea sweep through his weakened body; minds
He could not see opposed allowing him
To move upon the path he'd set himself.

The witch, he thought. She'd died. The dragon said
She'd died, but she had used the spirit bear
To forge a link out of the chaos wild
With death and nothingness and willed his will
To falter as she made the universe before
Him toss and turn, unstable, tipping ground.

How could I know what's going on? he thought.

And then he saw the spirit bear refracted
Out of his walking body on the snow.
His arm hair stirred with skin that tingled fear
Into the coldness of the snow and light.
He'd lost the battle that he'd thought he'd won.
He'd sent the bear into the nothingness,
But now he was Ruarther *and* the bear.
He was a monster walking on the earth.
He looked again and felt the shadow bear
Inside him as he walked across the snow.

What should he do? he thought. What could he do?
The witch and bear were locked in mortal combat,
And he was in the center buffeted
By forces greater than mortality
Could hope to face and still survive intact.

Two

Ruanne froze as her hand reached for a nail.
A vertigo so powerful it stunned
Her made her freeze upon the steep sloped roof
Where she was working on a shelter made
To hold a bowman who could shoot his arrows
When claws or fire came raking from the sky.

The voice that filled her mind was not the voice
Of Mmirrimann, but even larger, singing
With powers amplified by centuries
Of dragon elders taking care of dragons
In spite of all the awful human/dragon wars.
The dragon looked at her, evaluating
The woman that she was, and sighed so deeply
The sigh seemed dredged from all eternity.

"I am Ssruuanne," the dragon slowly said.

The golden dragon eyes blinked twice, and then
Ruanne was in the fields of blinding snow.
Ruarther, sheltering a spirit bear
Much larger than his body, eyes as red
As blood inside his veins, stood stunned, his life
Undone by knowing that he'd let the bear
Inside of him in spite of what he'd thought he'd done.

Without a thought Ruanne screamed out, "Ruarther!"
The village workers stopped their preparations
For dragon war and stared at how she stood
Upon the roof, her body aimed toward the mountains.

Ssruuanne conducted all the power streamed
Into Ruanne's wild cry toward Ruarther.
She shattered through the whirling chaos dancing
In waves around the hunter's muddled head.

Three

Ruarther felt a wave of raging love
Slam at the spirit bear inside of him.
He felt the bear's fierce spirit spit a spume

Of hatred at the cry that pierced it like
An arrow singing from Ruarther's bow.
He stood up straight. The winter air was clear
Of all the whirling making morning light

Miasmic, filled with chaos, hatred, loss . . .
He felt as if he'd found himself and shrugged
The forces centring into his body out
Into a universe he could not know or see.

He looked toward the mountains and the trees
He'd not seen lost inside the cold miasma.
They grew in clumps contrasting with the white
Reflecting light off snow upon the fields
That covered hills that rose into the cliffs
That soared above him sheer and rusty red.
He felt as if he were a child at night
Who was alone as dire wolves howled their hunger
Toward the darkness of an unseen moon.

A mile away a small stone cabin stood
Alone inside a wilderness that seemed alive
With songs too powerful for stone to silence.
He felt as if he'd starved himself for days.
He knew he'd reached the cottage that he'd sought
So angrily and single-mindedly.
He could not see the witch's child outside,
But smoke was rising from the cottage fireplace.
He knelt down on the snow and took an arrow
And notched it on the bow's taut, ready string.

He'd show the golden dragon that his heart
Was strong enough to mock her dragon fire,
He thought. He'd found the witch's child she'd tried
To make him save from winter's deadly storms.

~ 36 ~

Metamorphosis

When Wei woke up, she felt as if the fire
Inside the fireplace had gone out and left
The cottage icy from an outside wind,
But then she saw her mother glittering
Beside her deathbed, coldness pouring blue
From where her mother sat, its ice so bright
It made her mother shine, a radiant ghost.
Mysteriously, a fire was burning bright
Inside the fireplace even though hot coals
Were all that should have lasted through the night.

Wei sat up slowly, staring at her mother,
Fear cold inside her stomach as she felt
The fateful meaning of her mother sitting
So bright beside her bed, the whirling chaos
Emerging from another universe
An unseen cloud that filled the cold, bare room.
The minute Wei sat up her mother rose
And floated swiftly to the cottage door.
Wei pulled her boots on as her mother waited,
Then shrugged into her winter coat and rushed
To follow as her mother disappeared
Into the cottage's strong, rock-made wall.

She felt a patterning of power spark
Into the rhythm of her heartbeats, speeding
Her sense of time into a blur of light.

She opened up the door and went outside.
The morning sky was blue and bright, the snow
Reflecting light in waves of dancing air.
Her mother moved toward the springtime pond
Now sheathed with snow encrusted on its ice.
Wei hurried as the sparks of power surged
And made her feel as if she'd gained a life
Beyond the life she'd always lived, a song
That melded with the music of the stars.

Beside the pond her mother stopped and turned,
As sightless as a bat bathed blind with light,
And waited for her daughter as Wei crunched
Across the crusted snow, her heartbeats singing.
As soon as Wei was close her mother raised
Her shining arms and made a sure, swift motion.
Wei stopped and mimicked how her mother moved.
The light around her seemed to coalesce
Into a wave of fiery lines that burned
Their substance deep into the morning air.
Her mother turned toward the spot the sun
Rose up above the mountains, starting day.
The dragon scales on Wei's arm throbbed with heat.

She turned just as her mother turned and saw
The golden dragon rising from her cave.
A man was standing in her line of sight.
He had a bow inside his hands and stared at her
So evilly it almost made her flinch,
But then her mother made another motion,
Her arms a liquid movement streaming fire
Out of her substance bright into the day.
Wei waved her arms and saw the dragon etched
With rainbow colours in the waves she made.

It looked as if the colours from all dragonkind
Had flowed into bright bands of pulsing light.

She did not look toward her mother's light,
But waved her skinny arms again, as sure
Of how the spell should be as if she'd laboured
For years to master every nuance sung
Into the power of the art she made.
Her mother's form began to dissipate
And flow into the dragon's rainbow light.

Wei held her breath and felt a forceful surge
Of energy suck all the air out of her lungs.
Her mother's disappearance made her feel
A mourning just as sharp as she had felt
The day she'd pulled her mother's body down
Into the grave she'd dug beside the pond.
She mumbled incantations made of sounds,
Not words, and sang her breath into the dragon
That seemed to flow around her human form.

Another dragon, then another dragon,
Then scores of dragons left their mountain caves.
The sky filled up with dragons boiling bright
With colours from the mountain's rocky cliffs.
The hunter with his bow seemed stunned to see
The dragons and the witch's child together
In air alive with rainbowed turbulence.
He had an arrow notched, but could not seem
To force his arms to pull the bow's taut string.

Wei smiled and brought his frightened face
Close to her face, her body still as stone,
And then she moved her arms again and felt
Two rainbow dragon's hearts begin to merge

Into the beating of her single heart,
The drumming loud and painful, all the earth
And snow and sun and sky a unity
That knew no start or end, but spiralled out
Into the substance of the coming life-force.

She was the rainbow dragon, triple hearts
The song of who she was, the witch's child,
Transformed from human flesh to dragon flesh.
The pain she felt as bones began to grow
And shape themselves into a dragon's bones
Wracked through her body, made the stars that danced
In front of her a fire that belched from air
Into her skin and blazing dragon scales.
She whimpered as the pain grew more intense,
So hot it seemed to wipe away the day
And who she was, a little human girl.

Ssruuanne, above Wei's head, her wings a storm
Creating funnel winds of shining white,
Turned round and round as other dragons came
And grew so numerous the morning light
Dimmed from the thickness of their roaring wings.
The sky had metamorphosed wild with wings
And dragon bodies as a hurricane
Of dragons generated winds whipped harsh
Across the snow-bound landscape dark with storm
Stirred from a sky without a single cloud.
Stunned, terrified, Ruarther held his bow
And tried to understand the weirding loose
Inside the world, its singing powerful
Enough to make him feel invisible.

~ 37 ~

Determination, Doubt, and Dreams of Victory

Inside the cave he'd clawed in mountain rock
Sshruunak's resentment at the inconvenience
Of living rough outside the dragon lairs
Kept waking him, the cold intense enough
To make him wish he'd spent more digging time.
He kept on saying that discomfort made
Him miserable right now, but soon the moon
Would be invisible and then the song
Of dragon wings would beat so dreadfully
The earth would tremble from the flames of rage.

The thought of nineteen males and females
Now following his lead to dragon war
Seemed like a gift more precious than his hearts
Inside the small cave's dark, a bolstering
That made his plans more promising than he
Had dreamed that they could ever come to be.

Inside his head he saw his clutch of dragons
Spread out across the skies, their bodies large
Enough to make irrelevant the men
That scurried with their deadly bows and arrows.
He felt the power of their thundering
Inside his hearts and felt so potent-wild
He thought that he could burst out from his cave

And wrest the ancient stories from ancestors
And make them live in glory in this time.

But then the image faded as he thought
About the news his new force brought: Of Mmirrimann
And all the elders on the conclave's stone,
Especially Ssruuanne who'd let her mate
Assume her place upon the dais to call
For dragon war, great dragons battling dragons.

A male had not been on the dais, the sign of war,
For all the years he'd been alive. What did it mean?
The old ones' foolishness enraged him, made
Him want to spew his fire into their smug,
Old surety with force enough to make them cringe,

But still, his followers were young and strong . . .
But could they face the dragons from the caves?
Could victory be carved from dragons first
And then from humans with their puny strength?
What had he done? Created dominance
That would ensure that dragons lived without
The endless threat that humans represented?
Or made a war where dragon claws and flame
Raked mostly dragon hides and forced a slide
Into extinction Mmirrimann was fond
Of warning all the dragon caves about?

He'd trained the fearless males who'd followed him
In discipline and strategy, but now
His newer followers were here to join
The battle that he'd planned for carefully,
And though he'd lead his forces through the skies,
What would they do when dragons they had known

The moment when they'd left their eggs for light
Confronted them and came at them with flames?

He'd somehow thought the elders would sit back
And let him fight the humans in his war,
But if the dragons that had left the conclave
To join him in the mountains had it right,
His war against the humans was a part
Of what they faced, the other part a war
He had not planned or even contemplated.

His doubts gnawed at his stomach, made him want
To shriek his fear and helpless feelings out
Into the quiet night and make them vanish,
But if he showed his feelings to the others . . .

He'd heard the hesitancy in the way
The new ones told of elders at the conclave
And felt the cold dismay his males had felt
To feel the possibility of war
Fought with their fathers, mothers, sisters, brothers . . .

What could he do? he asked himself. What should
He do? He could not stop events from moving
So fast he had no choice but forward movement
Toward a destiny not guaranteed.

He thrashed inside the cave and cold, then moved
His wings. He left the irritating cave
For air that whistled as he flapped his wings.
Stars shined so brightly silver light rained fire
Upon the valley far below his flight.
Great dragon bodies moved uncomfortably
To hear him leave his clawed-out earth and soar

Into the crystal darkness of the night.

For hours the newest dragons had clawed earth
To make themselves a cave where they could sleep,
But mountain rock was hard, and days were needed
To make a cave, not hours before night came.
The mountain cold pierced through a dragon's scales.

Still, no one followed him into the sky.
One day to train the new ones how to fight
A war with strategy instead of rage,
He thought. Stoormachen and the others who
Had learned the tactics had to take the lead.
The clutch he led would not be quite as fierce
As what he'd dreamed when he had set his rage
Toward the moment when he'd wage a war
Against the hunter who had sent his arrow
To blind his eye and wrack him deep with pain,

But cowering was not the dragon way –
Not even if Ssruuanne and Mmirrimann
Were strong enough to fill the skies with dragons
Opposing him and what his mind had willed.

He drove his wings down, spurted higher, up
Into the thinner air toward the stars.
They'd win, he screamed inside himself. They'd win!
They had no other choice than victory.
The old ones wouldn't dare to test his strength.

~ 38 ~

Mesmerised Cave Dragons

One

Ssruuanne's cry ripped through Mmirrimann and jerked
Him upright in his cave, his whirling eyes
So bright they made the morning light seem dim.
He moved toward his ledge and launched in flight
Like other dragons from their sheer cliff caves.
The sky was filled with dragons, colourful
And urgent as they flew toward Ssruuanne.
Her cry had interrupted many dreams.

As Mmirrimann flew violently toward
The cottage where the witch's child was braving
The harshness of the winter's cold and wind,
He saw an image of Sshruunak, black wings
A smudge above the icy mountain peaks,
Imagining his victory against
Ssruuanne and Mmirrimann, his mind not yet
Aware of all the forces lining up
Against the brightness of his shining dreams.

Then, heartbeats wild, the ancient dragon felt
The place where grim shades gloamed inside the dusk.
He felt disintegrating history
As dragons failed into miasma's cold.
He almost plummeted to earth to see

Ssruuanne upon the ground beside a whirling,
Wild dance of colours where the human girl
Was changing from a human's frail, small shape
Into a dragon's powerful, full form.
The girl was melding spindly bones and flesh
Into hard scales that shined with rainbow light.
They caught the morning sun and danced and whirled
With making so unnatural and weird
It made him want to flee to memories
Where life was how it ought to be and weirding
Was more a legend than reality.

He roared so loud he thought he'd strained his lungs,
But then he heard the other roars surrounding
The place of transformation, heard the fear
That raged into the morning's clear, clean skies.
He spread his wings and landed as a hundred
Great dragons found a place to land on snow.

What madness had inhabited the world?
The dragons sat inside a massive circle
Around the human girl and felt her melding
As power danced out of her human heart
Into the thunder of a dragon's hearts.
As time coagulated, formed, then flowed
Into the swirl of being, nothingness
Around the rainbow human/dragon girl,
Ssruuanne began to hum deep in her chest,
Her song so deep it throbbed out of her bones.

Her song memed out into the other dragons,
Their voices oscillating through the snow,
The earth caught in the miracle arising
From where the nexus of the ether-world

Had linked into a weirding of reality.
The thrumming dragon song reverberated
Off mountain peaks and echoed through the caves
That sang the song into the valleys far
From where Ssruuanne and Mmirrimann sat stunned.
What madness had inhabited the world?

Huge dragons, rainbow coloured, like small hills,
Upon the whiteness of a winter's snows,
Around a rainbow swirl of burning light
Shaped like a dragon never seen before,
Hummed dragon songs that filled the universe,
The void where chaos born of swirling souls
Spun emptily past dragon memories.

Two

What have I done? Ruarther thought. I am . . .

The golden dragon that had made him run
Away from her so long ago came down
And landed in the snow beside the child
Transforming from her small girl human shape
Into a swirl of light now dragon shaped –
And then another dragon landed, then
Another, then another, wings so loud
It made him deaf to any other sound.

The dragons closed around him, breaths so loud
It made him feel as if he'd chanced a storm
Too powerful to live through if he stayed,
But not one dragon even looked at him.
They landed, whirling eyes fixed on the light
That burned a rainbow dragon's hearts alive

Into a life that could not really be.

The power of the dragon song throbbed potently
Into the air about him, a deadening
That turned his stomach inside out and seemed
To shake him to the core of who he was.
He staggered as a darkness overwhelmed
His sense of where he was and swept away
A deepness that he'd never felt before.
He tried to shout into the dragon's singing,
But as the darkness shredded, letting light
Alleviate a shade of darkness cowled
Around a place inside his self he'd not
Perceived before, he felt unmanned, as if
The world he'd known all of his life had changed.

Ruarther dropped his bow into the snow
And turned toward the forest evergreens
Around the cottage's stone-earthen walls.
He moved around the dragons one by one.
They did not threaten him or even see
That he was like a mote inside their midst.

He felt the emptiness inside of him,
The absence of the spirit bear who'd lived
Inside his body longer than he'd dreamed.
The bear had used his weakness in the woods
To gain attention when his fear had bludgeoned
His spirit with uncharacteristic shock.
He'd opened up his spirit by the campfire
And let possession soothe away his pain.
He'd thought he'd kept his spirit from the bear.
He'd banked upon a strength he did not have.
He felt inside himself and tried to know

For sure if he had shaken off the bear,
But how could he, a human, ever know?

He thought about Ruanne, her dark disgust
At how a man she loved could dream of killing
A child he'd never known or even met.
How could he have become that evil man?
What madness had inhabited his world?

The dragons did not frighten him or make
Him feel the way he'd felt the night the great
Black dragon had attacked him by the ledge.
He felt confused, afraid of who he'd been.

He stopped. He could not go back to the village.
He'd never wanted anything so badly
As grace enough to change the life he'd lived.
He felt as if the spirit bear were gone,
As if his spirit were his spirit once again.
He wanted to forget the witch's child
Burned like a brand inside his tortured spirit
And go back to the days when he had been
A hunter bringing game to feed his people,
Depending on the skills he'd honed from childhood.

What had he done? he asked himself. What darkness
Had made him think the evil that he'd thought?

Inside the trees he still manoeuvred slowly
Around the dragons mesmerised in snow.

~ 39 ~

The Song of Becoming a Dragon

Wei felt the light around her, felt her bones
And flesh expanding out toward the light.
She heard Ssruuanne above her flying, saw
The golden Old One stretch her claws to land,
But could not pay attention to the voice
That called to her, her flesh becoming light,
Congealing back to flesh that felt too heavy
For any human frame to ever bear.

The pain's excruciating twisting disappeared.
She felt no pain, although the singing fire
That rose up from her chanting voice created
An agony that seemed as if its roots
Were in the universe her mother's life
Was clutched in, struggling against the formless,
Cold winds that were no winds, miasma blank
Enough to be an element beyond
The understanding of an individual life.
She felt her spell, and light that flowed in rainbows
Out from her spell, solidify to bone,
Then dragon scales as bright as drops of sun.

She did not think, I am a little girl!
But felt her transformation as her head
Ballooned into a dragon's head, her heart
Into the double beating of a dragon's hearts.

Her hands stopped moving in their spelling dance
As wings grew on her back and arms and legs,
Became a dragon's massive arms and legs.
Inside her mind her mother sang as if
She'd left the nether world and fixed herself
Into the flowing of her daughter's thoughts.
Wei felt as if she were no longer Wei,
But more than Wei, a human, witch, her mother,
A dragon unlike any other dragon
Hatched from an egg upon warm hatching grounds.

Light hardened into flesh and scales and bones.
Her body seemed too large, unwieldy, awkward –
As if it were not who she was, but still
Was truly who she was, a spirit creature
Transformed out of a human to a dragon
Who had a witch's powers and a human's wiles
Imbedded in a child with dragon wings.

At first she only saw the light congealing
A rainbow storm inside her mind, around
Her body; then her hearts began to beat,
And then she saw out of a dragon's eyes,
The whirling strangeness of the world a bending
Of consciousness and even understanding.
She tried to move her massive dragon legs,
But saw her movement made the dragons gathered
Around her in the snow involuntarily
Move back from her, their fear of weirding strong
Enough to make them want to spread their wings
And flee into the freezing winter skies.

Ssruuanne and Mmirrimann walked forward, though,
Fear whirling in their eyes, but brave beyond

The ancient age that lived inside their bones.
Wei tried to move again, but felt as if
She were a baby still inside her crib,
Her movements larger than they should have been,
But human-sized, not fitting for a dragon.

Ssruuanne, her mind awhirl, sent thoughts
Into the rainbow dragon's mind, "Slow child,"
She said, awe in the song inside her thoughts.
"You have to take things slow until we know
What magic you have brought into the earth."

Wei looked at her, at all the dragons strewn
Like boulders on the fields she'd known so long.
She tried to find her mother's ghost among
More dragons than she'd ever dreamed existed.
She did not want to be a dragon, did
Not want to live a life that was not human.
She could not see her mother, could not feel
The humanness that made her who she was.
She was a girl, she thought. A human girl!

But still, she'd yearned toward this moment since
The day she'd dug her mother's grave and placed
Round stones above the body's emptiness.

Ssruuanne moved close and touched Wei's scales.
How could a human have a dragon's scales?
Wei tried to move again, but felt the awkwardness
Of never having been so large before.
She stumbled, then moved upright as the strength
Ssruuanne sent shocking through her body made
Her feel as if the light about her were her self.
The dragons in the field seemed so intense

With whirling eyes and primal fear she coiled
Away from who she knew she had become.

"Enough!" the thundering voice of Mmirrimann
Demanded calm. "We're dragons, not the spawn
Of emptiness," he said. "I've heard of this,
Of humans taking on a dragon's shape
And dragons taking on a human's shape.
We need to find the reason why this weirdness
Has come just as existence trembles where
Extinction and continuance are poised."

"Slow, child," Ssruuanne said once again. "You're not
A dragon, not a human child, but something else.
You're not alone. Both Mmirrimann and I
Are here; we'll find the balance that is you,
And then we'll understand this lunacy."

Wei moved her foot and slowly moved her wings
And let them fall back to her massive back.

"I need my mother who has died," she said
While looking at Ssruuanne's bright golden eyes.

Ssruuanne looked at the dragon child as large
As any full-grown dragon, but was silent.
As Mmirrimann stared at the rainbow fire
That seemed to pulsate from Wei's dragon scales,
He started humming, dredging up a song
Out of the depths of dragon memory.
Another dragon started humming too, and then
The mass of dragons hummed, an echo bouncing
Out of the caves that were their mountain home.
Wei startled. What was going on? But then her mother,

Inside the flesh that was her flesh, inside the dragon
That she had wanted to become, began
To hum just like the field of dragons hummed

She looked into Ssruuanne, her golden eyes.
She was a dragon. Born of light, her mother's
Deep human love for her had turned her life
Into a dragon's life. Her mother lived
Inside of her, inside the dragon that she was.

She glanced at Mmirrimann, Ssruuanne.
She felt her mother's humming, heard the song
Dredged from the ancient dragon memories.
She moved her massive legs and tested wings
That felt as if they could not be her wings.

And then, deep in her chest, she let the song
She felt come out of her so powerfully
It added music to the dragons' song.

~ 40 ~

The Mind's Black Fire

One

Inside her cottage, weary from the work
  She'd done with all the other villagers,
  Alone, the comfort of her rocking chair
Suffusing through the soreness in her bones,
She felt a sudden rush of fear and wonder
Infecting her with dread so powerful
It made her look around in panic.
She felt the dragons fleeing from their caves
And wondered if the war was suddenly
Reality, a monster wolfing human/dragon lives
And leaving devastation in its wake –

But then she saw Ruarther draw his bow
Upon a field of shining, endless ice
And saw his face dissolve into a mask
Of weird bewilderment, as if his life
Were ending as it spiralled on outside
The life he'd lived up to that moment's instant.
Inside her sewing room she saw him drop
His bow and lose the madness that had made
Him find the witch's child intending murder,
The spirit bear expelled, abruptly gone .

And then she saw him think of her, Ruanne,
And home and how he'd brought game home to help
The village live its life inside the forest

Where dire wolves came in winter and the dragons
Flew past so high they seemed mere colours specked
Upon the clearness of the endless skies.

But then she saw him stare into the whirling
Intensity of one great dragon's eyes
And felt him turn away from where he'd lived
His life in honour, flinching from the shame
He felt at having worked obsessively
To kill a girl he'd never even seen.
She felt him kneel in snow and start to search
for where his spirit could find peace again
away from weirding spirit bears and dragons
and even her, the woman whom he loved.

How could she see him? Not through dragon eyes,
Ssruuanne or Mmirrimann, but through a cord
Of spirit-sense that bound her heart to his
No matter how insane or evil he might be
In struggling against the demons fused
Into the human that he should have been.

She put her hand up to her mouth and let
A small cry echo through the sewing room.

But then she felt the sense of miracle
And fear inside the dragons spread across
The fields of snow outside the cottage where
The girl Ruarther's rage was aimed against
Lived lacking mother or adult for care.

What could she do? What should she do? The weirding
Was emanating waves of witch's power
Into the dormant depths inside her hands

And made her want to use the knowledge she
Had spent her life denying as the world
Swirled change and bridges to a place forbidden
Into a fabric never meant to be.

And then? And then? A distant, tiny spark . . .
A black fire seared into Ruanne and bounced
Into Ruarther, ricocheting off
The shields he'd built when exorcising forcefully
The spirit bear, into Ssruuanne whose eyes
Were drawn from Wei's mutation up
Into the skies above the mountain peaks.

A recognition of Ruarther flared
With hate so toxic that it made Ruanne
Sink to her knees upon the cottage floor.
She felt a dragon up so high its lungs
Were straining for each breath, its flight a rage
Containing promised death for humankind.

Ssruuanne's mind blocked the fire that scorched Ruanne.
Surprised, Ruanne heard screaming blistering
Into the cottage's small space and saw her door
Fly open as a half a dozen men
Came storming in to find out what was wrong.
The last man in was Cragdon whose pale face
Grew paler when he saw how Ruanne looked.

He gasped, "The dragon!" Then collapsed as if
He'd felt the black fire sizzling Ruanne.
"What's wrong?" an anxious Reestor ordered, voice
Commanding, filled with panicked dread.
The men around her looked like spirit beasts,
Their faces wavering with spirit light.

Ruanne searched frantically for normalness.
Bright rainbows seemed to dance before her eyes,
And dragon voices sang deep humming songs

What could she do? she asked. What should she do?
She felt the blackness in the morning skies.
She looked at Reestor, eyes so bright
They seemed as powerful as dragon eyes.
Outside a crowd had gathered, wondering:
Was war and death cusped in the flight of dragons?
Were all their dreams and hopes for life now gone?

Ruanne stared, scared, at Reestor's eyes and fought
To force the black fire and its burning hatred
Out of her mind into the wilderness.
She felt a dragon wheel above the earth
And hurtle like a stone toward the peaks
Where other dragons waited in the snow.

Two

Unhinged, afraid, she looked at Reestor, forced
Her voice to sound as if she were a woman
And not a witch who understood the dragons
And told him, "Leave," she said. "I need to think
Through what I've seen. You have to leave right now."
Objections sparked in Reestor's probing eyes.
The men behind him in the cottage stared
At him, then her, confusion in the way they stood.

"I need a moment, just a time alone,"
She pleaded. "I have got to understand
The vision in my head." She looked at Reestor. "Please."
As Reestor stared at her he didn't speak.
"Okay," he said at last. He turned around

And motioned to the men inside the room.
They muttered. In their voices fear was knitted
Into objections far too menacing
To voice where weirding made their hearts ice cold.
They turned and followed Reestor out the door.

Three

Alone, at last, exhausted from the villagers,
Ruanne lay on her bed. Her hands throbbed, pulsed
From energies she'd spent a lifetime fleeing,
But now she understood. The time of war
Had come, and in her mind were strategies
Inherited from mothers stretching back
Into the generations that had led to her.

She took a deep breath, sat up, and let the rhythms
Awakened by the dragon minds she'd touched
Wash over her, old powers dormant now
Alive with knowledge that she couldn't know.

She gathered up herself and prayed to Selen.
She got up from the bed and went outside.
She'd work with Reestor. Time was disappearing.
They'd need to work all night to be prepared.
She heard the men up on the roofs, their hammers
Creating nests for archers strong enough
To face the mindlessness of dragon rage.

A witch was welcome in a time of war,
But when the war was done? She mourned her fate.
She wove her hands and saw a rainbow dragon
Newborn inside the morning's golden skies.

~ 41 ~

To War! And Raging Dragon Hearts!

Above the earth, stars hard and bright against
The thin, cold blackness of the atmosphere,
Sshruunak felt faint from lack of oxygen.
The tug of gravity was powerful enough
To make him strain his wings to stay in flight –

And then he felt the weirding far below,
The swerve of history as rainbow light
Congealed into a dragon's hardened scales
Around the heartbeat of a human girl.
From Mmirrimann an image filled with dread
And wonder seemed to dance before his eyes.
The weirding somehow linked him to the dragon
He most feared in the world, the human man
Who was his enemy, and still some other human,
A woman sending out a web of linking.

He felt outside the ganglia of minds
That sparked into connections buried deep
In dragon memories linked back to times
When solitary power filled the hearts
Of dragons hid in solitary caves.
He felt a journeying that seemed outside
Of who he was, kaleidoscope of rage
Red-eyed, incensed that human brains could scurry
In bodies small as ants and still wrap him

With ropes that would not let him save himself.[6]
He felt the memories of Mmirrimann
Begin to sing into the rainbow light
That haloed round his stratospheric flight . . .

And then, his self alive inside the old,
Dark dragon's mind, his power surging out
Into connections not available
to younger dragons still involved in making
The self that would protect them from the songs
Miasma and the ancient memories
Could strike into a dragon's hearts, Sshruunak
Exploded with a black, cold rage that slammed
Into the human woman linking him
And Mmirrimann, the man who'd burned an arrow
Into his eye. A humming escalated, soared
From dragon spirits to a world upon the cusp
Of breaking from its egg into life's light.
He felt the woman fall, saw the human evil
Beside a dragon in the snow fall down,
And heard the grumbling rage in Mmirrimann
Distract the ancient dragon from the rainbow
Inside the field and force awareness, harsh,
To lock on Sshruunak's seething bolt of rage.

As Mmirrimann's awareness ricocheted
Back to Sshruunak, the younger dragon's wings
Collapsed, and suddenly he fell as if
He'd lost what strength he had to have to fly.
He plunged toward the cold, hard mountain peaks,
His rage so great he could not make his wings
Stretch outward, letting air support his weight.
He struggled as he fell and twisted, turned,
Until, at last, he forced his wings to flare

Into the thickening of air as flight
Came back to him and let him feel control
And let him flatten out his flight above
The earth and let him feel alive again.

The link between the dragons in the field
And him was gone, and in its place he saw
He could not wait for night to start his war.
A miracle had caught cave dragons deep
Into a rainbow mesh they did not understand.
He could not let them extricate themselves
If he and all his followers were fated
To ever rid the earth of human evil.

He aimed toward the valley where black stones
Were charred with dragon fire and flew so swiftly
The air around him whistled from his flight.
The light was growing in the sky as shadows
Retreated from the slowly rising sun.
He shot his urgency into Stoormachen.

"The war has come!" he screeched inside his mind.
"We've got to make the war unleash our rage!"

Stoormachen startled from the shallow cave
He'd dug into the mountainside and looked
Into the sky and tried to see Sshruunak.
He seemed confused, unsure of what dark threat
Had changed the plans Sshruunak had drilled in him.

"We have to move!" Sshruunak repeated, wild
With edginess, afraid delay would end
Up ruining all the dreams he'd brewed inside
Since arrows buried fire into his eyes.

"The dragons and the humans are distracted.
The plans have changed. We've got to hurry! Move!"

Stoormachen spotted blackness in the sky,
Sshruunak's flight swift enough to startle him.

The followers Sshruunak had gathered felt
A stirring in their spirits and their hearts.
They heard the urgency Stoormachen bleated
Into the mountain air and felt the fire
Of battle lust so suddenly inside
Their minds that they could barely see the boulders
Below them shining in the early sun.
They looked and saw Sshruunak's wild flight and moved
Their wings to greet their leader's urgency.

The time had come; the dragon's legacy
Of fire and claws and mindless rage had come!
They watched Sshruunak plunge like a meteor
Into the valley's eastern edge, his blackness
Contrasting vividly against blue skies.

"To war!" their leader roared. "To human death!
And fiery dragon flame and raging hearts!"

~ 42 ~

The Shock of Rage

The shock of rage from cold black dragon eyes
Stunned through Ruarther like a wave undoing
The man he once had been before he'd faced
Ssruuanne upon his hunt inside the forest.
A second sight surrounded him and let
Him see the spirit bear who'd governed him
Inside miasma holding who it was
Together with intensity of hate.

He saw the past, and how he'd cowered down
Behind the boulder with a frightened Cragdon
As black wings swooped from darkness at his life
And spewed out darkness in its raging hate
That wanted all humanity to die.

The dragon he had passed flinched azure scales
As blackness roiled into her mind and echoed
Into the other dragons in the snow
Around the rainbow human dragon, Wei.
Ruarther felt the threat inside the rage
And shook himself, the core of who he was.
He saw himself before the Old One, bow
Pulled back as terror raged inside of him.
He heard the Old One's pleading words that tried
To move him to compassion for a child,
And flinched to feel him send an arrow's flight

Toward a being who had meant no harm.
He felt the flame that blazed behind his back
And saw himself, as frightened as a deer,
Turn, run toward the deepness of the forest.
He'd never thought he'd ever be a coward,
But only cowards sought a spirit bear
So they could have the strength to leave themselves
And hunt a young girl child they could have saved.

He looked at where he was, his body pointed
Toward the capital where Clayton lived.
He felt his fingers on the bowstring taut
With death aimed at the rainbow that was once
A child and felt Ruanne inside his mind.
He felt the love she felt for him in spite
Of all the madness that she knew possessed
The man he once had been, and felt the bow
Fall from his hands into the plateau's snow,
The human dragon child, the rainbow dragon
Oblivious to who he was or why
He stood with deadly rage in front of her.

The chaos whirled around him as the bear
Discerned his presence in the roiling void
And lunged in desperation at the path
Now open to the earth he longed to find.
Behind him purgatory roiled like waters
That always probe toward a crack that can
Be widened to release a surging flood.

Ruarther did not flinch, but closed the path
Sshruunak had opened with his wave of rage.
He felt the fires and claws of war intrinsic
Inside the blackness that had made the dragons

Flinch from the rainbow miracle unfolding
In front of Wei's small house below their caves.
He touched the beard now overgrown from weeks
Without a razor, tried to understand
The cowardliness inside of who he was,
And felt depression's sapping, creeping slide,
As subtle as a snake inside deep grass,
Into his arms and thoughts that dredged a loathing
He'd banished from his life while still a child.

But then he squared his shoulders imperceptibly.
He had a task to do. He'd always been
A hunter who had brought game when starvation
Was in the children's haunted, frightened eyes.
He'd been afraid of dragon flame when he
Had failed to hear compassion in a dragon's voice.

He looked out at the dragons' craning necks.
They stared at skies as if they were afraid
Of what they'd heard proclaimed into the day.
He knew his enemy, the night-black wings,
The flame that seared his flesh and nearly sent
His spirit to the greyness of the void.

He could not face Ruanne or those he'd known
And fed for all the years he'd been alive.
He felt her as she warned the village, Reestor,
Of war launched from a mountain valley out
Toward the village where he'd lived his life.
He saw that he had always been conflicted
And turned the love he'd earned away and felt
Unspoken feelings not imagined by Ruanne.

He'd never make the village by the time

The warrior dragons started up their war.
No dragon on the plain's white snow had spread
Their wings and taken flight, but everywhere
Eyes searched the skies and waited as the wave
Of blackness dissipated in the air.

Ruarther looked at hands that held no bow.
They trembled slightly as he looked at them.
He turned toward the village, shrugged, and started
To run toward the home he'd always loved.
He hoped the dragons in the snow surrounding
The rainbow dragon did not mean to join
The war the night-black dragon meant to wage.
The village had no hope if all the dragons
Began to move against their human foes.

He had to pace himself; he had to try
To add his arms and wits against the storm
No human could escape once it had come.

~ 43 ~

Fate and Sentinels

One

As Cragdon stood upon the fieldstone wall,
   He felt a wind so cold it drove through flesh.
   He forced himself to hunch against the battering
That rolled from mountains, past his place
Upon the wall, into the village humans.
He strained to see the dragons in the skies
Ruanne had said were coming full of rage.
The men had taken up positions meant
To let them fling their arrows from a wall
That would not burn when dragon flame belched out.
The mothers had their children hidden, buried
Beneath large slabs of stone beneath the floors
Of cottages built when the dragon wars
Were devastating human/dragon lives.

He straightened up against the chilling wind
And thought about the blackness of the dragon
He'd fought beside Ruarther in the dark.
Inside Ruanne's small cottage, dragon eyes had slammed
Into his spirit, forcing him to fall,
But now he stood determined, stronger than
He'd been just weeks ago, a warrior armed
With weapons that he'd use to fight the evil
Swooped raging from a night-black silver sky.

The black-scaled dragon had possessed no way
To know Ruarther's mind, he thought, but still
Its actions, mirrored to Ruarther's rage,
Had hurled a war at humans at a campfire
Without a provocation in the night.

He felt the dragons even though he saw
No trace of dragons in the morning light.
He wondered how much guilt he had to bear
For deaths resulting from the coming war.

He shifted on the wall and tried to see
Beyond the distance walling in the sky.
He'd fought a dragon once, he told himself.
They'd not use claws and fires to devastate
Ruanne and all the men who'd sought him when
He'd stumbled through the blinding glare of snow.
He'd use what strength he had to shield his wife
And child against the possibilities
Horrendous in the wheel of human fate.

Two

The black rage boiled at Mmirrimann and stirred
His blood to mindlessness, Sshruunak's rebellion
A seething hatred as he turned away
From what the human girl had generated
Out of her mother's need and looked toward
The mountain skies where dragons rose to war.
Ssruuanne, beside him, stared at him in silence.
She stood beside the human rainbow dragon
And waited as he conquered mindless rage
And started calculating what response
Made sense as miracle confronted fate.

The other dragons, ringed around the girl
Transmuted to a dragon, seemed distraught,
Eyes shocked by feeling blackness ricocheted
Across the fields of snow, Sshruunak a nightmare
They'd thought would go away, but dreaded deep
Inside their inmost thoughts, rebellion woven
Into the history all dragons lived.
They seemed to hesitate as Mmirrimann
Decided what he'd do to meet the challenge
Sshruunak had sent into the dragon host.

"He'll end the dragon race," growled Mmirrimann.

"Responding will create a dragon war,"
Ssruuanne replied, her thoughts intense and sickened.
"No dragon's fought another dragon since
The Time of Mindlessness and Gorgon's fight
To build the strength of dragon sentience.[7]
We cannot fight the daughters and the sons
We saw break from their eggs into the light."

The rainbow dragon, still pulsating light,
Looked calmly at the two of them, her changing
Done, humanness a part of who she was,
A dragon on a field where other dragons were.
Her song was softer than a dragon's song,
Her voice so musical it had the sense
Of springtime winds whooshed through the leaves of trees.

"The dragon race will live," she said. "The war
Will not disgrace the strength of who you are."
She spread her multi-coloured wings and drove
Them downwards as she rose inelegantly
Into the air above the frozen pond.

Three

As Reestor lit the fires inside the pots
The men would use to light the arrows used
To splash flames over hardened dragon scales,
He cursed the day and said a heartfelt prayer.
Ruanne, beside him, said no word, but sparked
The flame into the pot he placed beside
Each man, eyes grim with fear and strength of mind.

He could not hear the children hidden dark
Beneath the cottages, but knew they cried
And pleaded with their mothers for their love
As life became a dream they'd never dreamed
Would change their lives while they were still so young.
He thought about the horror of his father's death
And wondered why the ancient horror marched
Alive into a time when wars were in the past.

He almost dropped the pot he held when flame
Flared up too high and almost singed his hand.
Ruanne just looked at him, still silent, scolding,
Eyes wild with brewing, devastating spells.

Unsettled, Reestor looked toward the wall
Where Cragdon and the others strained their eyes
To see the dragons flying at the village.
Someone would see them coming, shout their warning,
And life would change from what it ought to be,
And nothing would be as it once had been.

~ 44 ~

The Deadly Dragon Horde

One

Up from the mountain slopes above the circle
  Of black stone, dragons filled the sky, their hearts
  And spirits fierce with dragon rage and war.
Above them, eyes afire, Sshruunak watched fiercely,
Exultant that his time had come, the skies
So filled with rising dragons that they seemed
A swarm of blackness, death aimed at the humans.
The sun was bright and echoed off the snow.
He glided as they came to him, then turned
Toward the village closest to the caves
And shrilled his challenge at the universe.

Two

The blackness emanating from the mountains
Made Wei attempt to move her too-large wings
And lift herself into the morning air.
The snow around her sprayed and glittered light.
Ssruuanne moved quickly back to miss the force
Of wings more powerful than Wei could know.
The human child inside the dragon body
Felt tears well up inside her tearless eyes
As nothing seemed to move as muscles strained
To lift a body not her body off
The ground into the nothingness of air.

She moved her massive legs and beat her wings
And roared frustration, startling her hearts
That thundered in her chest and frightened her.

She was a child, she thought. She could not be
A dragon with a dragon's skills and hearts.

A little way away a wild-eyed Mmirrimann
Kept glancing at the sky and then at Wei,
His feet a drum-like tattoo on the snow.
He looked as if he did not know if he
Should launch into the skies or watch the rainbow
In front of him become a winged great dragon.
Around him, stretched as far as Wei could see,
The other dragons stared at Mmirrimann,
Then Wei, as if they waited for a sign
That told them what the black mind-storm assailing
Them meant inside a day of miracle.
Great dragon eyes whirled colours at the light
Intense enough to make the morning golden.

Ssruuanne was silent as the human dragon
Strained at the gravities of solid ground.
She looked confused, as if she could not make
Her thoughts reorder to reality.
At last, the struggle in her thoughts' confusion
So strong it made her feel more like a human
Than elder dragon born with dragon strength,
Ssruuanne reached out and touched Wei's dragon mind,

"On ground this flat you have to run to fly.
On cliffs you launch from ledges into air.
The question is, what are you flying to?"

Sshruunak's cry slammed its triumph through the plateau
As Wei began to run, her panic turbulent.
She lurched from one side to another side
As Mmirrimann and other dragons moved
Away from her and wings that did not match
The rhythm of her wildly churning legs.
Ssruuanne took off so smoothly, wings
A golden flashing in the light, she seemed
A definition of a dragon's grace.

Along the edges of the dragons' circle
A dozen other dragons leaped to flight.
Then Wei, her heartbeats double beating rhythms
Her legs and wings could synchronize, so slow
It seemed as if she'd slam into the ground,
Rose from the snow into the air in flight.
She murmured to herself to feel the wonder
Of being what she was, a dragon flying
From human form into the heaven's skies.

Around her dragons filled the air, so many
There did not seem the space to hold them all.
The blackness drumming at her mind suppressed
Exhilaration storming through her spirit.
She was a human dragon flying, strong
Enough to be the being she'd become!

And then she felt another cry, a human cry
That shivered where her arms had been and made
Her human heart asynchronous with how
Her dragon hearts beat with the beat of wings.
She gasped, a human, still a dragon. Fear
And anger made her stall, then start the beat
That kept her in the air again, the blackness

A song outside of who she'd ever be.

Three

Sshruunak's dark madness, Mmirrimann's fear
Of dragon lives forever lost in time,
Their glory, swirling eyes, intelligence,
Capacity for love between them lost,
Transcendent metamorphosis of Wei,
The sight of wings that seemed more light than membrane,
The memory of blackness from the wars
That decimated dragons as they strove
To claim old legends which were never real
Sparked deep into the dragons from the caves
Spread out across the field beneath the cliffs.
The human-dragon lurched into the air,
Wings pulsating scintillating colours.
Repulsion, fear, disdain for humans, love,
Respect for Mmirrimann, Ssruuanne, the dream
Community had sung into the spirit
Of dragonkind, exploded into sounds
Of dragon wings that lifted massive bodies
Into the morning skies, a following
Toward a war that should not, could not be.

Four

The coal-black dragon led the arrowhead
Of dragons flying at the waiting village.
His heart calm, Cragdon turned and shouted out
The warning that the village knew would come,
Then dropped behind the wall and took his bow
Into his hand and lit a flaming arrow.
There had to be more dragons in the clutch

Than he had ever seen in all his life.
Ruarther had not flinched to fight a dragon
By moonlight when the two of them had faced
What seemed to be a night of certain death.
Ruarther long ago had lost his self,
But Cragdon had a wife and child and love
And would not flinch to splash his arrow's flame
Into the hardness of a dragon's scales.
He waited, glanced to see the dragon's distance,
Then knelt behind the stony wall again.

Five

Ruanne, upon her cottage roof, heard Cragdon's voice
And knew the time of blackness came on wings
Of many colours as attacking dragons
Gave shape to darkened songs inside her mind.
She felt the power of their warrior song
And felt her witch's power stirring in response.
Come on, she thought. Come on. We'll meet you here.
She lit the pot. It leaped with flame. She yelled
Defiance at the coming dragon horde.

~ 45 ~

Not the Only Enemies

One

The dragon's shadow over Cragdon chilled
The ground beneath his feet and made him quail
Beneath the hugeness black above his head.
He dipped his arrow in the small pot's flame,
Moved from the wall, and let the arrow fly.
The coal-black dragon of his nightmares roared
So loud it shook the ground as flame splashed wild
Across the scales too hard to penetrate.
Without a moment's hesitation Cragdon
Pulled back his bow's string, sent another arrow
Into the dragon's tail, and saw the dragons
Descending on the village, crowding skies.
He did not falter, sent another arrow
Toward the violet dragon following
The one-eyed leader of the dragon phalanx.
The arrow hit the dragon's massive chin
As wild green eyes aimed claws at Cragdon's body.
The roaring seemed as if its decibels
Could shake apart the village cottages.

Two

Ruarther heard the drumming sound of wings
And turned to see the golden dragon's claws
Extended, glittering, toward his shoulders.

He cursed, remembering he'd lost his bow,
And stumbled as the claws descended, grabbed
His deerskin jacket, lifted him above
The ground, heart frozen by his terror, mindless
As rabbits shadowed by an eagle's wings.

"Calm down," Ssruuanne demanded. "In the end
You did not kill the girl or use your bow.
You'll never reach the battle on your own."

The voice inside his head was large enough
To make him feel as if he were a bit
Of flotsam in a stream in early spring.
Below him trees and open fields rushed past.
He'd travelled days to pass such swaths of land.
The steady beat of dragon wings filled up
The world with songs unknown to human beings.

Beside the two of them, invisible,
The spirit bear roiled whirls of empty air,
Time, no-time interplaying with the beat
Of time inside the dragon's song of wings.

Inside herself, Ssruuanne examined why
She'd picked the weak-willed hunter from his race
Toward a battle that would end before
He'd even heard its roars and anguished screams.
The man had disappointed her, she thought.
He should have tried to save the girl and stop
The madness now unleashed into the world.
Why had she swooped so low, once spotting him,
And lifted him, with her, into the air?
She'd lived so long, but still was puzzling
The being that she was inside her scales.

She felt the hunter was important. Why?
The question was, how could a coward be
Important in a time of deadly war?

Three

Sshruunak aimed at the cottage where thoughts streamed
So clear into the morning air they seemed
A clarion call of all humanity
And what the humans meant to dragonkind.
Each slate grey tile upon the cottage roof
Seemed etched into his brain as wings
Drove down into the air and rushed his rage
At what had troubled him since pain had flared
And bled his eye away into the night.

He felt Ruanne upon the cottage roof
And heard the hum of murmuring that meant
She thought her spells could send him spiralling
Into defeat that left the humans strong
Enough to end the dragon threat forever.

He roared, his roar so loud and deafening
It shook the ground below his hurtling flight.
He sent a stream of angry flame toward
The roof where Ruanne hid behind a shield
Of slate designed to shelter her from flame.
He felt his followers behind him, roars
A symphony of rage from dragon throats.
They'd feed on human flesh before the day
Had ended in a blood-red light of fire.
A blazing, burning brand of flame splashed pain
Across his tail's hard scales and made him flinch
Away from where he'd aimed his fire of death.

The minute that he flinched, near to his head,
Another archer came out from his shelter, aimed,
And sent another splash of fire into his scales.
The air seemed filled with fire so thick the pain
It caused made breathing difficult and rasping.
He pivoted in air and crashed his bulk
Into the cottage nearest where he was.
The wall he'd smashed collapsed in front of him.

More flame engulfed his scales. He roared again
And beat his wings into the air; a human
Fell off the roof his bulk had smashed apart.
It looked as if it were a broken doll.
Around him dragons boiled above the cottages.
Each one had flames splashed on their hardened scales,
And everyone was fighting waves of pain.

He wondered where the discipline he'd taught
Had gone as dragons crashed their bulks at walls
The way he'd crashed his bulk into a wall.

They could not lose. He would not let them lose,

But then he felt the wings of Mmirrimann,
A swiftness flung toward Sshruunak's black war.
He had forgotten. Human enemies
Were not the only enemies they faced.

~ 46 ~

The Dire Wolves

One

The dire wolves, eyes as glittering as suns,
    Began to gather in the hills and forests,
    Great packs that knew of human/dragon wars
And salivated at destruction where
They would relieve the earth of carrion.
Upon the crest of hills they started howling,
Their songs a haunting madness shivering
Their ravening into the day's cold skies.

As Wei kept labouring to stay in flight
The voices of the wolves caused her to rise
Above the tallest treetops, dragons flanked
Around her as they rose up from the ground
And filled the skies with coloured scales and wings
That thundered as they flew toward the village.

How could a little girl be who she was?
Wei thought. The scales of light she wore outside
The human dragon that she was perturbed her,
Although she also held onto her sense
Of self inside the weirding of her life.

Beside her Mmirrimann kept humming songs
That seemed much older than the winter skies.
They seemed to reach into a time before

Time found its measuring, its arrow's flight.
Below the two of them Ssruuanne swooped down
And grabbed a human in her massive claws
And lifted him into the winter skies.
His frightened yelp was faint inside the beat
Of steady dragon wings that sent the horde
Toward the village Wei had left while young.

A pack of dire wolves burst out from the woods,
Their movement slow compared to dragon flight,
But filled with bristling energies that sang
Of violent spirits empty of remorse.

Two

Toward the mountains, distant from the flight
Of dragons, huge, a wall of mist began
To anvil up into the day's bright sky.
It poured into a crack made in the bridge
Between the nothingness of death and life.
Inside the mist miasma whirled and sparked
As if it held a winter lightning storm.
Shades gloamed in dusk as chaos sang and gates
And boundaries began to shift and fray.
Inside the storm, inside her daughter's spirit,
Wei's mother, father waved their witching arms
And blotted out the shine of winter sun.
Wei felt them struggling against the storm
Wei's transformation opened as a bridge
Between the realms of limboed death and life.

Three

Ruanne could feel the storm. The great black dragon,
His claws extended, hurtled at the shelter
She calmly nestled into; strong, grey slate exploded,
His body's strength so large it took away
Delusions of her safety, hammering
The cottage roof a half a dozen yards
Away from where she'd hid. She sent a bolt
Of energy out of her frightened spirit
Toward the massive dragon with his one good eye.
She felt another spurt of energy
Mesh with the bolt she'd sent, the two bolts strong
Enough to knock the dragon off the roof.

The dragon roared, crescendoing his voice
Into the muttered roars that punctuated
The battles flaming just above the rooftops.
She did not think, but notched a burning arrow,
Then sent it at a violet dragon's scales.

Four

Knocked to the ground, Sshruunak could feel the horde
Of dragons in the air, their eyes and necks
Strained at the melee in the war's first skirmish.
He wondered at the feelings forcing him
To understand that all his plans were dashed,
And, like the night he'd lost his eye, his life
Was spinning to a grim reality
He'd not perceived in shining, foolish dreams.
He pounded wings into the sky and searched
For dragons flying to the humans' rescue.
A bright light burned before the flying scores

Of dragons humming ancient warrior songs.
The rainbow of the light was much too bright
To countenance. What did the rainbow mean?
Behind its fire the skies above the mountains
Roiled spirit beasts and chaos to the world,
The cloud of nothingness a gate that promised
Extinction Mmirrimann had laboured to avoid.

He saw his followers were scorched by flames.
The burning underneath his scales seared pain
Into his mind's slow, sluggish desperation.
What should he do? he thought. What could he do?
He could not, would not lose the war he'd made.

Five

A shock made Wei forget to keep her wings
In motion navigating currents flowing
Above, below her shining dragon body.
Ruanne's thoughts rang in Wei and made the world
Seem brighter than the possibilities that trembled
As dragons filled the skies with who they were.

Wei saw the battle through Ruanne's wild eyes.
The great black dragon fell and then was up
And raging at his puny human foes.
His followers were shaken by the fires
That gouged into their scales and weakened them.
Where did the fires that penetrated scales
Impenetrable as cold iron come from?
How had the humans found a weapon
They'd never had in any war before?

Wei sent her dragon human powers deep

Into the stream of power emanating
From where Ruanne sat dazed upon a roof
As roaring captured all the world in pain.
A surge of power palpitated out
Of her and linked to where her mother anchored
Upon the ledge inside miasma bridging
The universe of chaos and reality.
She was a child, she thought, a girl caught up
In storms too big for her to understand.
She'd thought the dragons were immense enough
To banish fear and raging storms, but now
She saw a violet dragon on the ground
Caught in the throes of violent, painful death.

She felt her mother's and her father's surge
Of anguish as the curtain separating
Reality and chaos started leaking
A storm of spirit beasts, chaotic winds
That were no winds, but whirlpooled nothingness,
Into the world she circled, staring through
Ruanne's wild eyes and frightened, angry heart.
Behind her in the wild miasma's storm
The universe seemed like a madhouse thrown
Into a time where time did not exist.

Sshruunak's attacking dragons felt the song
That Mmirrimann, Ssruuanne, the others sang.
Wei flew beside her dragon kin and felt
Her mother's spelling at the boundary
Where all eternity and history
Spun on the cusp of change so powerful
No being would be like they were before.

~ 47 ~

Confrontation

One

Ruarther stopped his struggling inside
   The golden dragon's claws. They did not bite
   Into his flesh or even make him feel
Uncomfortable, although the ground below
Sped by so fast it made his stomach churn.
He looked at how the other dragons flew,
Their eyes intense upon horizons set
Beyond his human sight, and looked in wonder
At how the human dragon, with her scales
So bright with rainbow light it hurt his eyes,
Flew like the dragons flew, her wings a steady
Beat, driving her toward the village where
Her father's death had made her mother flee.

The spirit bear was just behind him, surfing
An eddy from the world of whirling vortex.
He wondered how he felt the bear inside
A storm he knew was there, but could not see.
Behind him weirding, bridging life and death,
Swirled madly in the morning's sunny skies,
A song unnatural within the world,
A wrongness brought to life upon a day
Unlike another day from history.

Ruarther held his self, inside the talons,

Inviolate from spirit bear possession.
What was a human man, who'd lived the wrongness
That he had lived, do when a dragon grabbed
Him, lifted him to flight, and let him live?
He looked toward the human rainbow dragon
And wondered why he'd been fanatically
Determined that she had to die if humans
Were destined to continue in the village?

The cold miasma following their flight
Was nightmare wild, sheer madness troubling
The sanity of shining morning skies.

He kept himself as still as possible.
The golden dragon's flight was way too high
To fall from if he valued living life.
Without a weapon, what role could he play
If he was dropped inside the village fighting
Against the ravages of dragon war?

Two

The clashing din of war was obvious
Before Ssruuanne could see the devastation
Where dragons battled villagers with fire.
Then Mmirrimann's wings started moving faster.
A violet dragon, Sshisshiton, who'd left
The conclave he had called to end the madness
Sshruunak had generated from his rage,
Was on the ground, her wounds so great she drooped
Her head and did not look to see the sky
Completely full of dragons from the caves.

The tension in her lover's flight reflected

The deadly sounds of battle now so loud
They seemed to inundate the universe
And silence even wildness in miasma
That followed them toward the tragedy
Now raging at the human's small stone village.
Below her dire wolves howled to smell the blood
Of wounded dragons and their human foes.

Then Mmirrimann roared louder than he'd known
That he could roar. The other dragons echoed
The power inside Mmirrimann as dragons
Aflame from burning human arrows danced
In skies and plunged toward the human archers
That bent their bows and sent their deadly flame
Into the scales of dragon hides, pain roiling
Both dragons and the humans as they died.

A dragon flung a human archer high
Into the air as roaring filled the skies.
Miasma's silent roar of sound entwined
Into the battle's roar, the dragon's roaring,
And seemed to leap toward the chaos raging
Above the cottages and forest trees.
Deep in Ssruuanne she felt the prophecy
That Mmirrimann had said in conclave, warning
About extinction for the dragon race.
She keened her sorrow at the sight of dragons
And humans battling toward their deaths.
Her keening made Ruarther, held by talons,
Squirm, trying to escape her talons' grip.

Enraged, an ancient dragon male who'd led
The mountain dragons during all their years
Of peace inside the caves, a hurtling Mmirrimann

Flew like an arrow at Sshruunak's black scales.
The coal-black dragon felt his leader's charge
And turned toward the threat he'd never thought
He'd have to face, his belly scales on fire,
His pain and rage so great the world seemed red
And violent in a mind unhooked from thought.

Miasma flowed toward the battlefield.
Once living spirits teemed and swirled in clouds
Of mourning, searching for the living light
Where absolution could absolve their spirits
Of darkness and the flowing cauldron central
To individuality's privation.
The earth quaked in the shivering blood-calls
From dire wolves' gleaming, hungry, dull red eyes.

~ 48 ~

Before the End of the World

Ssruuanne swooped suddenly toward the ground.
Ruarther closed his eyes and forced the cry
Of terror in his throat to swallow bile.
And then the golden dragon let him fall
A foot into the snow, his eyes still filled
With dragons smashing cottages as fire
From arrows burned their bellies and their sides.
The image of the ancient dragon that had flown
Beside the golden dragon from the field,
Descending on the coal-black dragon who
Had almost killed Ruarther in the moonlight,
Seemed false, impossible to understand.

Unharmed, he got up on his feet and saw
The stone wall circling the village, warmth
Inside of him as memories of life
He'd often treated badly, even though
The villagers, his kin, had honoured him,
Came rushing in a flood of wondrous joy.

He ran toward the wall, climbed up, and stopped.
Below, his face a frozen mask, was Cragdon.
His blackened skin had peeled to show his skull.
He'd died an agonising death by fire.
Ruarther sat, stunned, on the wall as dragons
Attacking dragons with ferocity

Reordered everything he'd thought through life.
The golden dragon that he'd feared so much
Roared down on Ruanne's cottage, claws extended.
The monster black that Cragdon and Ruarther
Had fought screeched as it rose to meet her claws.

What madness had possessed his life and made
Him choose a rationality so wrong
It had no anchor in reality?
He saw the bow that Cragdon once had held.

Above him spirit creatures, freed from chaos,
Streamed through the air toward the awful carnage
As dragons joined the humans fighting dragons.
The villagers, confused, had stopped their efforts
To launch their flaming arrows at hard scales
Since they could not discern which dragons fought
Beside them or against them in the battle.
The dragons wheeled and roared and filled the air
With coloured scales, wings, flames, and aerobatics.

Behind the wall of spirit beasts a storm
Swirled from the centre of a cloud that fell
In blackness down toward the snowy earth.
Ruarther heard the dire wolves howling rage
Before the storm and saw a wall of chaos
Inhaling light, normality, and reason.
The bridge between the netherworld and life
Raged worse than any dragon's roar or flame or claws.

Ruarther did not flinch to see the storm.
He'd lived through frightening storms too many times.
He glanced again at Cragdon's grimaced face,
Then stood upon the wall again, his face toward

The storm about to swallow up the world.
Why had a man as brave as Cragdon died?
Ruarther, tortured by his history
Of grievous faults, would not run from the storm,
But face its fury with a fury of his own.

Before the wall of swirling, ugly clouds,
The rainbow human dragon wheeled around,
A shining dragonfly against the deadly
Immensity the world could not escape.
Ruarther wondered at the grace he'd sought
So long to murder in his spirit-heart.

~ 49 ~

Retreat

One

The great black dragon's hurtling unnerved
   Ruanne, but, even though she felt like leaping
   From roof to ground and hiding with the children
Beneath the floors of cottages in dark,
She pulled her bow and sent a flaming arrow
Into the dragon's scales and saw him flinch
Back from the flame, his searing breath-flame missing
Where he had aimed, his claws a shrieking screech
Across the roof as wings fought hard to take
Him back into the air away from where she knelt.
Inside her mind she chanted words that seemed
As if they'd come from someone else and sang
As if her chanting had a power far
Beyond the power that she knew she had.

She felt triumphant for a moment seeing
The dragon swerve away from searing flames,
But then he turned and aimed his massive body
At where she pulled upon her bow's taut string
And hurtled at her smallness as she threw
Herself away from where he'd aimed, her arrow
Another flame into his hardened scales.
The dragon roared. Ruanne rolled down the roof
And tried to keep from plummeting to ground.
Her eyes filled with a sky of dragons so huge

The world seemed mad with frightened screams and roars
That shook the ground and made her feel half deaf.

"Undo the chaos of the universe,"
She sang. "Cleanse winds that are no winds.
Undo the chaos; stir the winds; make
The world anew, chaotic rage undone.
Undo the chaos of the universe."

She did not stop the chanting in her mind
In spite of all the bruising that she felt
While desperately attempting to arrest
Her rolling on the hard slates on the roof.
She did not stop while hanging from the edge
Above the ground, her arms afire with pain.
She dropped to earth and rolled to ease the fall.
Her voice wrapped dragon roars and human screams
Into the chant she sang and tried to end
The fury overwhelming what the village
Had once been, slumbering inside its peace.

She was no witch, she told herself, and still
She chanted witching words and reached for power
She'd never wanted, always shunned and fled.

Two

Sshruunak felt Mmirrimann before he saw
The dragon horde above the village walls.
He threw himself toward the chanting witch,
Then turned as Mmirrimann came roaring down,
His claws extended as he tried to pierce
Sshruunak's black scales and end the village war.
Sshruunak avoided Mmirrimann and tried

To understand the madness boiling skies
Alive with dragons fighting dragons, flame
And claws enraptured by the constant roar.

He'd never felt that Mmirrimann would lead
The caves to war against their sons and daughters.
His calculations had been wrong so often
That, even caught by rage, he knew his judgment
Was flawed so badly that he could not trust
The thoughts or feelings that were driving him.

He saw the human witch drop to the ground,
But then Ssruuanne was diving at his wings.
He twisted as another flaming arrow
Unnaturally burned through his dense black scales.
He'd have to fly. His followers would have
To fly toward the mountains where their lairs
Could not be found without a dogged search.
He roared, his pain so great it echoed like
A writhing snake into the village skies.

He started climbing, pumping wings in spite
Of how the flames upon his belly spread,
But then began to hover as he saw
The weirding clouds beyond the village wall
And dire wolves gleaming in unnatural light.
He saw the ending of the world of dragons
Foretold by Mmirrimann, despair so great
Escape was, like his life, like dragonkind,
A fantasy impossible to comprehend.
Fear clawed into his double hearts and made
Them beat arrhythmically, the chaos singing
Inside the roiling clouds so powerful
It overwhelmed his sense of what he was.

"Retreat!" he shrilled. "Retreat and fly away!"

His followers, disorganised and fearful,
Too many injured from the human's arrows,
Began, as one, to climb above the battle
They'd started following Sshruunak's black rage.
The fear Sshruunak had broadcast shocked their wings
Into a frantic flight toward the clouds
That boiled toward the village, whirling doom,
An ending, at the world that once had been.

~ 50 ~

Living Inside Chaos

One

The dire wolf woke Ruarther from his daze.
A male as large as any that he'd seen,
Eyes red, fur ragged, black as moonless nights,
Snarled, bold, into the opening between
The stone fence where Ruarther stood and woods.
It saw Ruarther, crouched in hunting stance,
And stared at him, its baleful eyes twin cauldrons
That bubbled hatred, blind ferocity.

Ruarther jumped down from the wall and grabbed
The bow from Cragdon's lifeless hands and sent
An arrow at the wolf in one smooth motion.
The wolf, wise to the wiles of men, moved sideways,
The arrow burying into a tree.
Ruarther pulled the bow again and aimed
At where he thought the wolf would move to dodge
His arrow's flight; the wolf howled; other wolves
Began to come out of the forest trees.
The wolf dodged sideways once again, but true
To how Ruarther's aim had been, the arrow
Imbedded sharpened iron in flesh; the wolf,
Now maddened, blindly charged toward Ruarther.
Ruarther sent another arrow deep
Into the charging wolf's dark heart; it fell
As other wolves howled rage that shivered

Into the roiling clouds behind their movement.

The chaos sang its silence at the earth.
A coldness colder than the fiercest storm
Rolled to the wall and poured into the village.
The howling voices of the wolves were silenced.
Ruarther heard the spirit bear, who'd tried
To occupy his body, in the cold.
It sniffed at him, then sniffed at Cragdon's body,
Then turned toward the village as a dark
That was no dark descended on the world,
A promise of an ending for all life.

Two

Above the battle Wei kept circling
As humans sent their flaming arrows splashing
Across hard dragon scales and dragons fought
With dragons as the village cottages
Caught fire and filled the air with smoke and flames.
She felt the chant Ruanne was singing deep
Inside her spirit, the song so powerful
It seemed to alter how time's arrow moved
Across the day toward night's distant rising.

Each time she wheeled to keep herself aloft,
She saw the clouds of chaos moving like
An anvil, dense as molten iron, toward
The village, humans, dragons, and the war.
She felt her mother's and her father's songs
Inside the chaos, felt her mother buried
Inside her human-dragon's triple hearts.
They strained to close the breach the winds
Of chaos blew into the mountains, down

The slopes toward where death fed frenzied wolves.

Extinction swirled inside the freezing clouds.
Wei felt the message from her mother's singing,
The strangeness of her voice inside of her
And still, somehow, inside the nothingness.
A dragon flying through the air, she longed
To feel her mother's loving, human touch
Upon her cheek before her mother tucked
Her gently into bed, the long day done.
But she had lost her childhood when her hands
Had woven dragon flesh around her spirit
And made her more than what she should have been.

At last, the boiling clouds intense with cold
Near village walls, she joined Ruanne's strong chant
And started moving it away from dragons
That spewed their fire toward her slender body,
Toward the chaos threatening the lives
Of every creature, every tree, on earth.
The surge of power as she linked her voice
To Ruanne's voice was startling; she flew
Toward the anvil-threatening clouds and reached to find
Her mother's and her father's core in chaos,
Their struggle as they tried to make an order
Inside a universe that knew no order.

She flew into what seemed impermeable.
Her mind was buffeted by winds so strong
And cold they numbed her sense of who she was
And almost knocked her from the skies she flew.
Her scales seemed like they would dissolve in cold
And flow into the winds that were no winds,
Her spirit part of nothingness that hurled

Its nothingness around for all eternity.

How could she live inside the nothingness?
The stream of chanting from Ruanne dissolved
Into a song so small she hardly knew
That it still tied her to the world beyond
The grey that sucked at her and tried to meld
Her spirit with the fleeting hints of life
That flowed and merged into the whirlpool-flow
That mocked the order that her parents sought.

Deep in her self, beyond the human dragon
That she had made, she reached toward a song
Beyond her individuality.
She tried to find the hearts of who she was
Beyond the being that she was, the truth
Of how life's impulse strained against the chaos
Imbedded in existence, making possible
The beauty and the substance of the world.

Three

Ruarther faced the cloud and cold and felt
The raging storm of nothingness unman
Him from the human man he had become.
He did not flinch, but reached into the place
That let him throw the surging spirit bear
Away from who he was and meld his essence
Into the spirit of the self he was.

The chaos storm's noise roared into his flesh
And numbed the beating of his human heart.
The cold bit down into his will and sucked
Determination from the spirit that he was.

He turned toward the village, feeling nothing
Inside the dark that raged around his body
And tried to feel his way toward Ruanne.
She had to be alive. His love for her,
Denied so often in his stupid pride,
Was strong enough to will that she still lived.

~ 51 ~

Upon the Brink of Destruction

One

Sshruunak and all his followers began
To flee the village. Mmirrimann sent out
A panicked plea to stop. Ssruuanne had swerved
To miss the ground near where Ruanne was chanting
Her power song and started following
The beaten dragon horde toward the chaos
That swirled its void around the village walls.

"Join with the witch's singing!" Mmirrimann
Demanded. "Find a balance for the world!"

The realms of death swept over cottages
And sang its chaos deep in sentient minds.
Ssruuanne wheeled in the sky and linked her mind
Into the song Ruanne was singing, coldness
Numbed deep beneath her scales into her hearts.
She felt how power flowing from the singing Wei
Had linked into the words Ruanne was chanting.
She felt the search that Wei was making lost
Inside the storm of nothingness, the flotsam
Of spirits, once alive, a ghostly dance
That swirled into the living universe
And started disassembling existence.

As Mmirrimann's strong spirit joined the song

And other dragons found the stream of beauty
Entwined into the grace Ruanne had made,
The chording of the music found the fear
In human/dragon hearts and grew until
The silent sound formed bubbles that surrounded
The village and the forest and the lives
That gave the earth its meaning laced in time.
Reality, assaulted by the winds
Of death, rose out of humans, dragons, trees,
And shimmered as another war erupted,
The chaos trembling over all of life
As life fought back with sentient hearts and song.

Below the floors where children hid from dragons,
Their mothers held their small ones close and tried
To ward away the chilling cold with love.
Inside the caves where guardians hovered over
The clutches of warm dragon eggs, stunned dragons
Reached out to find the song Ruanne had started
And tried to use the warmth inside the song
To keep the eggs from crumbling to mist.

Two

Ruarther tried to move his legs toward
The cottage wall he'd almost reached when mist
Descended over him and took away
Reality from eyes and touch and smell.
He felt the spirit bear, still whole, beside
Him, looking for a way into his physicality,
But, like he'd done inside the weirding wood,
He drove into himself until he felt
The song Ruanne was in his life and started
The process of building who he was from scratch,

His burning core alive inside the deadness.

He could not feel his movement through the mist,
But still he struggled, pushing out from deep
Inside himself into the world he knew existed.
Then, like a hint of morning light before
Light filtered dusk into a cloud cloaked sky,
He thought he heard Ruanne, her sweet, strong voice,
Outside his head, but still inside his mind.

He reached for her and fell into abyss
As dragon minds and human minds were linked
And sung as loud as any symphony
Had ever been at any human time.
The power of the mind-song slammed his heart.
He even felt the song sung by the stones
That only moved inside eternal time.

He moved inside the sound until he found
The chanting of Ruanne's sweet voice and joined
His voice to hers and wove a melody
Of two inside the strands of music weaving
Defence against the terror of the void.

There needs to be some certainty in life,
He thought. Inside the certainty is love.

~ 52 ~

The Long Song Done

One

Ruanne's, the dragon's, song gave strength to Wei.
   She moved her wings inside the nothingness,
   Ignoring wisps of spirits straining past
The place she'd occupied while still alive.
She felt her father, mother, in the void,
But only saw the swirling spirit ghosts
That danced and disappeared in currents stronger
Than any sense of being in a mind.

As other humans joined the song Ruanne
Sang with the dragons, Wei began to feel
A tide that seemed to have a substance absent
From hurricanes of empty spirits flung
About within the coldness of the void.
She spread her human dragon wings and forced
Herself to move into the feeble tide,
Its current stronger as she moved against
Its force, its substance growing grainier.

The song of life Ruanne had brought alive
Surrounded her and gave increasing strength
Until, at last, she saw them in the greyness,
Her father's and her mother's arms alive
With weaving substance out of vapoured absence.
The universe was dying in her world.

The sentience inside the trees was shorn
Of time that let them draw their sustenance
From earth and rich, black soils. The beating hearts
Of dragons and of humans boiled their essence,
Outside the power in Ruanne's wild song,
Into the nothingness hidden by a veil
Millennia had held until the day
Wei's mother's love had reached beyond her grave
And made the weirding storm now powerful
Enough to end all living on the earth.

Wei drew the song life sang into her hearts
And sang her love toward the substance holding
Her mother's and her father's selves together.
The chaos roared inside her ears and self.
It seemed as if the nothingness had gained
A life and hated anyone who threatened
To end the substance it had gained by feeding
On spirits vibrant in their realness.
The buffeting of cold assailing Wei
Began to draw her from the doorway where
Her mother wove her spells into the world.

Wei gathered up the song of life and hurled
It, filled with all she was, toward her mother.
Her mother's form, so ghostly in the void,
Became as solid as the love that tucked
A blanket to her daughter's chin at night
And let her daughter know the safety knit
Into the certainty of mother's love.
Her father touched her mother's arm and shook
His ghostly head and waved toward his daughter.

Receding, Wei saw sadness in her mother's eyes.

Her mother reached toward the power song
Surrounding Wei, and then the substance built
Inside a place where substance could not be
Began to dissipate into reality.
The dire wolves howled beneath the canopy
Of forest where they lived their ravening.
The hearts of dragons thundered as they flew
Above the village smouldering from war.

Wei saw her mother die a second time.
She would not visit as a ghost again.

Inside the dusk of chaos tattering
Into the substance of a normal sky
Grief wailed into Wei's triple hearts and shivered
Across the snow plains to the mountain peaks.
She felt her wings dissolving in the air.
She did not care, she thought. She did not care.

Two

The Old One felt the shift inside the chaos.
She spread her wings and tried to see where Wei
Was in the ending of the weirding storm.
A cleansing, bitter wind was blowing hard
Down from the mountain peaks into the village.
She strained her wings into the shrieking wind.
Behind her, Mmirrimann was following.

She saw the rainbow dragon sparking light
Into the darkness scattering away
From where the rainbow bands were shooting out
Across the surface of the wintered earth.
Wei's light was tattering apart the darkness

That swirled eternity inside the storm.
Ssruuanne felt that she might not be in time.
She flew much faster than she'd ever flown.
The rainbow dragon detonated light
Into the darkness as the sky turned blue.

A child fell from the light toward the earth.
Ssruuanne swooped low and grabbed the child
Inside her claws and climbed back to the sky.
Ruanne's song drifted off into a silence,
Her long chant done; her strength gone from her heart.

Beneath Ssruuanne Wei did not try to move.
She breathed, but did not seem to be alive.

~ 53 ~

Being Human

The morning sun was shining on the cliffs.
　　The dragonflies were swarming on the pond.
　　The surface of the pond seemed like it had
An ever-moving veil upon its face
As tiny multi-coloured bodies whirred,
Their wings invisible as bodies darted
A dance too intricate to figure out.

Ruarther came out of the woods, two hares
Limp in his hands, a light inside his eyes.
Beside the shed Ruanne stopped feeding chickens
That pecked around her feet and fluttered wings
And looked toward Ruarther with a smile.

"We'll need the hares!" she called out. "Reestor's sure
To get here near to dusk and supper time."

Ruarther's right arm lifted up a hare.

"I'll get them ready for the pot," he said
And walked toward the cottage's oak door.

Above them, using wings to brake her speed,
Ssruuanne flew past the cottage, neck outstretched,
And landed heavily upon the ground
Beside the pond and fleeing dragonflies.

Ruanne flipped up her apron, scattering
The seed into the air as chickens squawked
And flapped their wings, excited by the food,
And walked toward the golden dragon's shining.
Ruarther altered course and walked to join
Ruanne as warmly whirling dragon eyes
Looked at the two of them approvingly.

Behind them, from the cottage, Wei ran out
And shouted as she ran toward the three of them.

"Ssruuanne!" she called. "You're here! At last you're here!"

Ruarther dropped his hares upon the ground
As Wei ran up between them, smiling wildly,
And took their hands and skipped toward the dragon,
Her joy impelling them toward the pond.

"A human child needs human care," Ssruuanne
Declared approvingly. She reached out, touched
Her nose to Wei's small hand, and rumbled joy
Deep down inside her chest, her dragon sense
Of life a wave that rippled out into the day.

Ruarther did not say a word, but reached out, touched
His daughter's arm, Ruanne hugged close to him,
And felt how lucky he had been to live
Into this moment when he was a human man.

Notes

1. Lewis, C.S. 1961. *A Preface to Paradise Lost*. London: Oxford University Press.
2. From Davis, Thomas. 'Before the Time of Dragon Wars', an unpublished poem from *The Dragon Ballads*.
3. Lethe refers to a river in Hades, the realm of death, in Greek mythology. If a human crossed the river they forgot about the life they had lived and all they had loved and known.
4. This passage was inspired by Jonathan Edwards' famous sermon, 'The Future Punishment of the Wicked Unavoidable and Intolerable', delivered in 1741.
5. From Goethe, von Johanne Wolfgang. 1808. Scene IV of *Faust, Part I*.
6. From Davis, "Old Galrug", an unpublished poem from *The Dragon Ballads*.
7. A reference to 'Before the Time of Dragon War', another poem from '*The Dragon Ballads*'.

Bennison Books

Bennison Books has four imprints:

Contemporary Classics
Great writing from new authors

Non-Fiction
Interesting and useful works written by experts

People's Classics
Handpicked golden oldies by favourite and forgotten authors

Poetic Licence
Poetry and poetic works

Bennison Books is named after Ronald Bennison,
an aptly named blessing.

Bennisonbooks.com

www.ingramcontent.com/pod-product-compliance
Lightning Source LLC
Chambersburg PA
CBHW061637040426
42446CB00010B/1460

9780999007709